RAND

EDITORS: CARRIE M. FARMER,
KAYLA M. WILLIAMS, MEREDITH KLEYKAMP

BRANDON F. DE BRUHL, R. GORDON RINDERKNECHT,
SHADDY K. SABA, JULIA VIDAL VERÁSTEGUI,
JENNIE W. WENGER

The Role, Effectiveness, and Sustainability of Nonprofit Organizations That Provide Employment Support for Veterans

For more information on this publication, visit **www.rand.org/t/RRA1363-10**.

About RAND

RAND is a research organization that develops solutions to public policy challenges to help make communities throughout the world safer and more secure, healthier and more prosperous. RAND is nonprofit, nonpartisan, and committed to the public interest. To learn more about RAND, visit www.rand.org.

Research Integrity

Our mission to help improve policy and decisionmaking through research and analysis is enabled through our core values of quality and objectivity and our unwavering commitment to the highest level of integrity and ethical behavior. To help ensure our research and analysis are rigorous, objective, and nonpartisan, we subject our research publications to a robust and exacting quality-assurance process; avoid both the appearance and reality of financial and other conflicts of interest through staff training, project screening, and a policy of mandatory disclosure; and pursue transparency in our research engagements through our commitment to the open publication of our research findings and recommendations, disclosure of the source of funding of published research, and policies to ensure intellectual independence. For more information, visit www.rand.org/about/research-integrity.

RAND's publications do not necessarily reflect the opinions of its research clients and sponsors.

Published by the RAND Corporation, Santa Monica, Calif.

Library of Congress Cataloging-in-Publication Data is available for this publication.

ISBN: 978-1-9774-1430-4

Cover: Kemberly Groue/81st Training Wing Public Affairs, U.S. Air Force

About This Report

Nonprofit organizations play a significant role in the ecosystem of support for service members during their transition to veteran status and the civilian job market; their efforts have likely contributed to veterans having lower unemployment rates than nonveterans for several years. While this support is essential, we know very little about which organizations and which employment models are especially effective in supporting veteran employment. And at the same time, there has been concern about the sustainability of the veteran nonprofit sector as a whole, which could threaten the continued sustainability of effective organizations that support veteran employment.

RAND researchers sought to describe the landscape for nonprofit organizations that are providing employment support to veterans, provide a framework for measuring and assessing the nonprofits' effectiveness, describe the philanthropic environment in which these organizations operate, and consider how public-private partnerships might help to ensure that high-quality organizations providing effective employment support to veterans can continue to fulfill this important mission. Overall, recent trends in revenue and public opinion about philanthropic donations for this sector were strong; however, strengthening public-private partnerships could diversify funding streams and increase long-term sustainability among organizations the government relies on for services. Furthermore, efforts to expand and standardize measures for evaluating program effectiveness and impact would allow valid comparisons across different nonprofit programs, increasing transparency for veterans, funders, government partners, and the public.

RAND Epstein Family Veterans Policy Research Institute

The institute is dedicated to conducting innovative, evidence-based research and analysis to improve the lives of those who have served in the U.S. military. Building on decades of interdisciplinary expertise at the RAND Corporation, the institute prioritizes creative, equitable, and inclusive solutions and interventions that meet the needs of diverse veteran populations while engaging and empowering those who support them. For more information about the RAND Epstein Family Veterans Policy Research Institute, visit veterans.rand.org. More information about RAND can be found at www.rand.org. Questions about this report or about the RAND Epstein Family Veterans Policy Research Institute should be directed to veteranspolicy@rand.org.

Funding

Funding for the institute was made possible by a generous gift from Daniel J. Epstein through the Epstein Family Foundation, which established the RAND Epstein Family Veterans Policy Research Institute in 2021.

The research described in this report was funded by The Heinz Endowments, which seeks to help southwestern Pennsylvania thrive as a whole and just community and, through that work, to model solutions to major national and global challenges.

Acknowledgments

We would like to thank The Heinz Endowments for the generous grant that supported this research. We are grateful to the interview participants for their time and expertise, to Rajeev Ramchand for his insightful feedback, and to Phil Carter and Laura Werber for their thoughtful reviews.

Summary

Each year, more than 150,000 active-duty U.S. service members embark on a new journey as they reintegrate into civilian life. Among the biggest challenges many face first is securing meaningful employment. While all job seekers can likely identify with the uncertainty that accompanies a job search, veterans face specific challenges. First, veterans may be unsure of how their military knowledge, skills, and experiences match with the qualities employers are looking for. Moreover, it may not be clear what kinds of positions veterans are qualified for or which companies offer such positions.

In response to the elevated rate of unemployment among post-9/11 veterans (enlisting after the terrorist attacks of September 11, 2001) relative to nonveterans (Figure S.1), many nonprofit organizations and initiatives have been stood up to help get jobs for newly transitioning veterans. Although veteran unemployment rates are much lower since 2011 and, in fact, even lower than rates for nonveterans (Figure S.1), more than 150,000 individuals leave the military every year, meaning transition assistance is needed consistently, whether or not there are deployments, conflict, or recessions that may intensify needs.

Transitioning service members seeking help finding jobs often turn to nonprofit organizations to make up for a shortfall in such assistance provided by the federal government. Although the federal government spends more than $13 billion annually to support the transition from military service to civilian life (Kleykamp et al., 2024), the vast majority of this funding is dedicated to education benefits for transitioning service members and their families. The federal government spends comparatively little on employment support for new veterans. Hundreds or, perhaps, thousands of nonprofit organizations currently fill this gap and play an ongoing role in helping new veterans find jobs and helping other veterans with job transitions. While this support is essential, we know very little about which organizations and which employment models are especially effective in supporting veteran employment. At the same time, there has been concern about the sustainability of the veteran nonprofit sector as a whole, which could threaten the continued sustainability of effective organizations that support veteran employment.

FIGURE S.1
Changing Rates of Unemployment: Veterans and Nonveterans

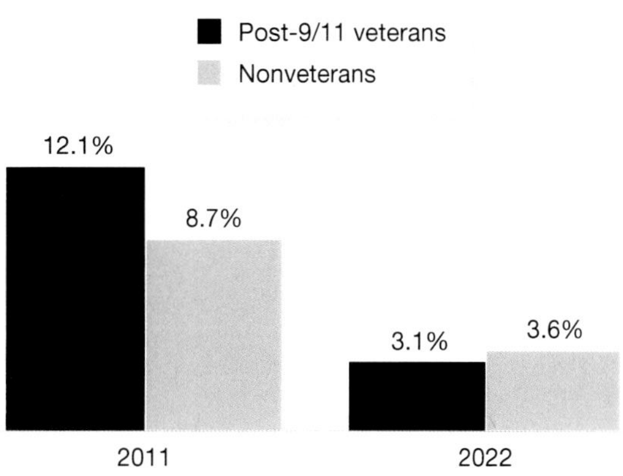

SOURCE: Features data from U.S Bureau of Labor Statistics, 2012, 2023.

We sought to describe the landscape for nonprofit organizations that are providing employment support to veterans, provide a framework for measuring and assessing the nonprofits' effectiveness, describe the philanthropic environment in which these organizations operate, and consider how public-private partnerships might help to ensure that high-quality organizations providing effective employment support to veterans can continue to fulfill this important mission.

We conducted a mixed methods study to address these aims. This consisted of interviews with nonprofit organization leaders, a review of selected organizations' annual reports to identify existing metrics of effectiveness, and a review of possible avenues for enhanced public-private partnerships as exemplified by other sectors. To assess the financial viability of these organizations and veteran-serving organizations as a whole, we also reviewed veteran nonprofit tax data and administered a survey to a representative sample of the American public to assess where veteran-serving organizations fall in their charitable giving preferences.

Key Findings

Although veteran unemployment is lower than nonveteran unemployment, many veterans who are transitioning still face challenges finding meaningful employment.

Although Figure S.1 shows a significant decrease in veteran unemployment in 2022, not all veteran groups fare equally well. For example, Black and Hispanic veterans have higher poverty and unemployment rates and lower household incomes than white veterans. Female veterans, despite having higher educational attainment than their male veteran peers, earn significantly less. Junior enlisted personnel are less likely than officers to already have a civilian job lined up prior to separation, and some military jobs, such as those in the infantry, involve skills that are hard to translate into civilian positions. Younger veterans, particularly those ages 18 to 24, have significantly higher unemployment rates than older veterans. Veterans as a group are doing well, yet there are still many veterans who find it challenging to transition into civilian careers and, thus, require assistance securing employment.

Veteran-serving nonprofit organizations often supplement federal transition programs and initiatives, especially in providing individualized employment services.

Nonprofit organizations that aid veterans seeking civilian employment after military service are a critical part of a larger veteran transition ecosystem. For example, the U.S. Department of Defense's near-mandatory three-day Transition Assistance Program helps transitioning service members understand their U.S. Department of Veterans Affairs (VA) and U.S. Department of Labor (DoL) benefits and how to begin to develop a résumé and job search strategy, while many nonprofit organizations have stepped in to provide individualized employment services, such as how to develop a specialized résumé and a personalized job search strategy. Such individually tailored services are especially important for veterans who face the greatest challenges transitioning into a civilian career.

Veteran employment nonprofit organizations often monitor and assess their inputs and outputs but do not use common metrics of program effectiveness.

It is extremely difficult to compare the efficacy of veteran-serving nonprofits. All nonprofit organizations participating in the study reported that they use input and/or output metrics (such as the number of participants or the number of sessions completed). Many also reported participant outcome data (such as job placements) to demonstrate the value of their programs to veterans and their families. However, there was an inconsistent use of measures across organizations, which hinders comparison studies. Furthermore, few organizations assess program effectiveness. Most current metrics focus on the *number* of veterans placed in a job, rather than any measure of whether it is a "good job." Efforts to track longer-term employment outcomes after initial job placement are limited. Without a set of consistent and standard metrics of program inputs, outputs, and outcomes, there can be no assessment of program effectiveness and impact and no valid comparison across different nonprofit programs.

Veteran-serving nonprofit revenue appears strong, but some traditionally large organizations are experiencing declining budgets.

Recent trends in revenue for veteran-serving nonprofits are strong. Internal Revenue Service (IRS) tax filings showed strong sector growth between 2016 and 2022. Growth for the entire charitable sector was only 8 percent over this time frame, while revenue growth for the top ten nonprofit organizations classified as serving military and veterans (IRS code W30)—including large organizations that often provide grants to smaller organizations with narrower areas of focus, such as employment—grew much more over the same period (34 percent). The top ten organizations assisting veterans with employment also had greater revenue growth (17 percent) than the larger nonprofit sector.

However, some organizations saw substantial—in some cases, dramatic—declines in revenue (Figure S.2). This was particularly true for traditional 501(c)19 veterans service organizations (VSOs), which can lobby for legislation that could benefit veterans, such as establishing new government grantmaking programs to fund effective veteran employment programs. This may be why some advocates and organization leaders express concern about the financial sustainability of these organizations in a shifting environment with less public visibility for veterans' issues and other issues competing for philanthropic resources.

There is opportunity for more-diverse financial support for nonprofit organizations that assist with veteran employment.

Many organizations that provide employment assistance to transitioning veterans rely heavily on corporate and foundation grants—thus, diversifying revenue sources could enhance their sustainability. The federal government is one potential source of funding. Many nonprofit organization leaders told us that their programs accept referrals from federal partners but do not receive funding from the federal government to provide services. Instead, much of the collaboration between governments and communities in the veteran sector is relatively informal. More-formal arrangements could allow the government to encourage, support, and sustain efforts in priority areas within the veteran transition space.

FIGURE S.2
Percentage Change in Revenue Among Nonprofit Organizations, 2016–2022

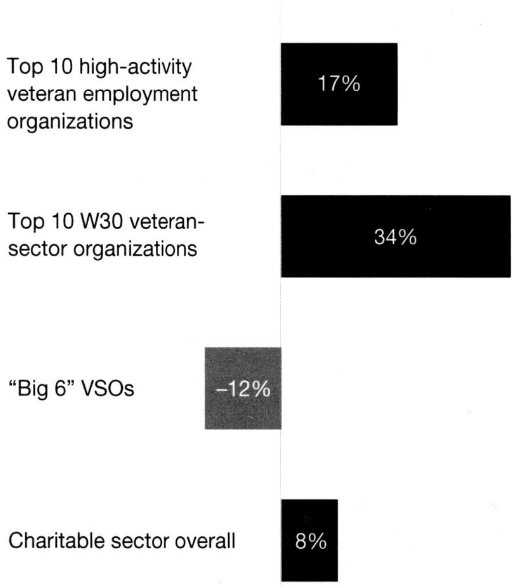

SOURCE: Author analysis of data from Candid, undated.
NOTE: "Big 6" VSOs are the American Legion, American Veterans (AMVETS), Disabled American Veterans, Paralyzed Veterans of America, Veterans of Foreign Wars of the United States (VFW), and Vietnam Veterans of America.

Individual giving is another source of funding and is a traditional source of support for nonprofits. We found that American adults strongly support veteran charities, and individual sentiment about giving to veterans' charities is on par with other issues of public concern. Overall, 14 percent of respondents reported donating to support veterans' issues in the past year, which is similar to or above other causes, such as climate change and social justice. Those who had a personal or family connection to military service were more likely to support veterans' charities. Respondents reported almost universally that they expect to donate at similar or greater rates in the future. Most agreed that private charitable giving to veterans' issues is an important supplement to federal funding.

Increased collaboration between government and the nonprofit sector could serve the public good in supporting veteran employment, but challenges need to be acknowledged and addressed.

Public-private partnerships hold promise for improving the efficiency and sustainability of veteran-serving nonprofits, though our analysis found that these arrangements can be subject to several types of challenges. To be successful, public-private partnerships must address issues around administrative and financial burden, information asymmetry, and principal-agent dynamics. For example, DoL's Employment Navigator and Partnership Program, which refers veterans to nonprofit partners for employment assistance, faces challenges of financial burden and information asymmetry: Participating organizations supporting veteran job placement and information are not directly funded by this program, yet the government relies on these organizations to have sufficient resources to place veterans who are referred. To address these challenges and ensure the effectiveness of these partnerships, the government should compensate nonprofit organizations at a market rate for services they provide (e.g., job placements) but also collect performance information to ensure program objectives are met.

Recommendations

Given the essential role the nonprofit sector plays in supporting transitioning service members, improving the veteran-serving nonprofit sector's effectiveness and sustainability for the future is critical. Our analysis suggests several key recommendations.

Federal Agencies

- **Increase transparency about public-private partnership programs to reduce information asymmetry.** Federal agencies responsible for public-private partnerships should ensure clarity and transparency about requirements, administrative overhead, and decision criteria for grants, which should be clearly articulated in the rulemaking process to improve information resolution and accountability.
- **Appropriately fund nonprofit partners engaged in public-private partnerships.** Federal agencies should properly account for the value being provided by the partnerships by creating incentives for meeting the terms of contract or service agreements. Incentives should be at a market rate at which the nonprofit partner can sustain the program.
- **Require veteran employment–focused organizations that receive federal grant funding to report in a standardized way on a common set of program process and outcome evaluation metrics.** This can increase transparency and accountability and suggest where more effort is needed. Consensus should be reached on what measures to include and how to define them by seeking input from DoL and VA advisory committees and then publishing the proposed measures and their definitions to solicit public comment. Funding should offset the added costs associated with this requirement.
- **Consider a long-term strategy using a "whole of government" approach to support public-private partnerships for transitioning service members and veterans.** Such a strategy could include flexible, per-client grants that include service eligibility and reporting costs, allowing transitioning service members to access and transfer funds between providers. In addition, developing cost-sharing tools and a unified data strategy would improve transparency and reduce transaction costs.

Corporate and Foundation Donors

- **Require grantees to use similar metrics.** Along with promoting transparency and accountability across veteran employment–focused organizations, metrics can assist in decisionmaking based on program outcomes and impact.
- **Develop a definition of a *high-quality veteran employment organization*.** Once developed, criteria for high-quality and effective organizations can be used to determine which organizations to support.
- **Support additional research on underemployment.** This should include the establishment of a measurable definition of underemployment and analyses to understand the extent of this problem among veteran and nonveteran populations. Investments in

research on underemployment would help improve monitoring of program effectiveness and overall trends through time.

Veteran-Serving Nonprofit Organizations

- **Identify opportunities to participate in public-private partnerships.** Partnering with federal agencies by applying for relevant grants and contracts could provide a novel revenue source and potentially stable source of funding. However, organizations should be aware of administrative and other costs of participation.
- **Consider direct appeals for philanthropic support.** There is strong public support for veteran-focused initiatives. Direct appeals to the public could increase revenue and diversify funding streams.

Contents

About This Report ... iii
Summary ... v

CHAPTER 1
The Role of Nonprofits in Veteran Transition ... 1
Kayla M. Williams and Meredith Kleykamp
Background ... 1
In Brief: How This Study Was Conducted ... 3
Veteran Unemployment: How Good or Bad Is It and for Whom? ... 3
Assessing the Role of Veteran-Serving Nonprofits in Employment ... 5
How This Report Is Organized ... 6

CHAPTER 2
Views of Veteran-Serving Nonprofit Leaders ... 7
Meredith Kleykamp, Kayla M. Williams, Julia Vidal Verástegui, and Shaddy K. Saba
Methods: Interviewee Selection, Interview Protocol, and Data Interpretation ... 7
Major Themes from Nonprofit Organization Representatives ... 9
Conclusion ... 12

CHAPTER 3
Measuring Program Effectiveness ... 15
Jennie W. Wenger and Julia Vidal Verástegui
Current State of Measuring Effectiveness of Nonprofit Veteran Employment Organizations ... 16
Framework for Identifying and Standardizing Metrics ... 21
Conclusion ... 23

CHAPTER 4
Veteran-Serving Nonprofit Finances ... 25
Shaddy K. Saba and Kayla M. Williams
Financial Data and Analytic Methods ... 26
Trends in Philanthropy ... 27
Funding Flows in the Veteran-Serving Nonprofit Sector ... 28
Employment-Focused Veteran-Serving Nonprofits ... 30
Conclusion ... 33

CHAPTER 5
Public Sentiment on Charitable Giving to Support Veterans ... 35
R. Gordon Rinderknecht and Meredith Kleykamp

The RAND American Life Panel: Data and Methodology ... 36
Charitable Giving Behaviors ... 37
Attitudes Regarding Charitable Giving to Veterans ... 37
Factors Affecting Charitable Giving Decisions ... 39
Conclusion ... 40

CHAPTER 6
The Role of Public-Private Partnerships to Support Veteran Employment ... 45
Brandon F. De Bruhl
Evaluating the Modern Public-Private Partnership Typologies ... 46
Considerations for Current and Future Public-Private Partnerships to Support Veteran Employment ... 51
Conclusions ... 52

CHAPTER 7
Conclusions and Recommendations ... 55
Veteran-Serving Nonprofit Revenue Appears Strong, but Sustainability May Require Adaptation ... 57
Identifying High-Performing Organizations Requires Improvements in Measurement and Reporting ... 58
Public-Private Partnerships May Be an Opportunity to Enhance P3 Ecosystem Sustainability but Need to Address Partnership and Information Challenges ... 59
Limitations ... 60
Conclusion ... 61

APPENDIXES
A. Interview Participants ... 63
B. Interview Codes ... 65
C. Additional Interview Findings ... 67
Meredith Kleykamp and Kayla M. Williams
D. Tools for Program Management, Planning, and Evaluation ... 71
Jennie W. Wenger
E. NTEE Codes ... 75
F. IRS Designations for Veteran-Serving Nonprofit Organizations ... 77
Kayla M. Williams and Shaddy K. Saba
G. American Life Panel Survey Supplement ... 81
R. Gordon Rinderknecht and Meredith Kleykamp
H. Evolution of VA's P3 Ecosystem ... 87
Brandon F. De Bruhl

Abbreviations ... 93
References ... 95

Figures and Tables

Figures

S.1. Changing Rates of Unemployment: Veterans and Nonveterans v
S.2. Percentage Change in Revenue Among Nonprofit Organizations, 2016–2022... viii
4.1. Veteran Unemployment and Number of Active-Duty Separations Annually Versus Revenue to the Sector (2022 inflation-adjusted dollars).......... 33
5.1. Proportion of Respondents Who Donate to Each Cause 38
5.2. Preferred Sources of Funding for Veterans' Issues 39
5.3. Attitudes Regarding Which Veterans' Issues Should Receive the Most Charitable Giving 40
5.4. Attitudes Regarding Which Kinds of Veterans Should Receive the Most Charitable Giving 41
5.5. Respondents' Anticipated Future Giving to Veterans' Issues 42
5.6. Most Important Factors Affecting Respondents' Charitable Giving Decisions.... 43
6.1. Challenges by P3 Type 50
D.1. Example Logic Model 73
G.1. Proportion of All Giving That Goes to Veteran Issues Among Those Who Give to Veterans' Issues 81
G.2. Proportion of Respondents Who Donate Each Dollar Amount 82
G.3. Most Important Factors Affecting Respondents' Charitable Giving Decisions, by Expanded Giving Categories 83
H.1. Punctuated Equilibrium Model View 91

Tables

3.1. Comparisons of Program Effectiveness Are Not Possible Because Organizations Report Different Metrics 17
4.1. 2022 Revenue and Expenses of Top Ten W30 Organizations (by Revenue) 29
4.2. 2022 Revenue and Expenses of Top Ten W30 Employment Organizations (by Revenue) 29
4.3. Revenue of Top Ten W30 Organizations in 2016 and 2022 30
4.4. 2022 Revenue of Ten Employment or Leadership Development Veteran-Serving Nonprofits 31
4.5. Revenue and Revenue Change in Employment Organizations and Other Subgroups (Using 2022 Inflation-Adjusted Dollars) 34
6.1. Typology of P3 Organizations 47
6.2. P3 Challenges by Type, Based on the Extant Literature 53
B.1. Interview Codes 65
G.1. Demographic Overview and Supplemental Measures (%) 84

CHAPTER 1

The Role of Nonprofits in Veteran Transition

Kayla M. Williams and Meredith Kleykamp

Background

Each year, more than 150,000 active-duty U.S. service members embark on a new life chapter as they reintegrate into the civilian world. For many, a critical first step is finding gainful employment. Job seekers from all walks of life can likely identify with the uncertainty that comes along with the search for a new position. But years of research, bolstered by veterans' own stories, have demonstrated that veterans are tasked with a tough additional step: They must translate their military expertise, skills, and experiences into the kinds of proficiencies valued by employers. In addition, transitioning veterans enter a job market that is unfamiliar to them, and it may not be immediately clear which positions are suitable or what companies might offer relevant positions.

That many veterans need assistance in finding employment was made clear in the years of the Great Recession. The U.S. Department of Defense (DoD) spent $1.0 billion on unemployment compensation for ex-servicemembers in 2011 (Congressional Budget Office, 2017) as unemployment peaked for post-9/11 (after the terrorist attacks of September 11, 2001) veterans at 12.1 percent. This was significantly higher than nonveteran unemployment (8.7 percent), which was considered high. It was also higher than the unemployment rate experienced by veterans who served before 9/11 (8.3 percent) (U.S. Bureau of Labor Statistics, 2013).

It became clear that new efforts were needed to support veterans who were unemployed and looking for work. First Lady Michelle Obama and Jill Biden mobilized support from diverse stakeholders and pulled together the Joining Forces initiative, which brought public, private, and nonprofit organizations together to tackle unemployment among veterans and military spouses; other priorities included education and wellness (White House, undated). The U.S. Chamber of Commerce Foundation formed Hiring Our Heroes (HOH) (U.S. Chamber of Commerce Foundation, undated). Eleven companies, including JPMorgan Chase, Verizon, and Cushman & Wakefield, committed to hiring 100,000 veterans by 2020 as part of the 100,000 Jobs Mission. Since then, the initiative has grown to encompass more than 300 companies with an expanded goal and remit (Veteran Jobs Mission, undated).

Efforts such as these were accompanied by federal policy and program changes. In 2009, veterans were added to the Work Opportunity Tax Credit Program, and the Veterans Opportunity to Work Act of 2011 launched a major redesign of DoD's Transition Assistance Program (TAP) curriculum and made participation mandatory with some exceptions (H.R. 2433, 2011). The National Defense Authorization Act for fiscal year (FY) 2019 mandated additional changes to TAP (Pub. L. 115-232, 2018), including a revised core curriculum and optional tracks for employment, higher education, vocational training, and entrepreneurship. As of 2022, more than 90 percent of transitioning service members participated in TAP annually (U.S. Government Accountability Office [GAO], 2022). (For more information on federal transition programs, see Kleykamp et al., 2024.) With this combination of public, private, and nonprofit effort, along with the strengthening of the nation's economy, unemployment among post-9/11 veterans fell to 3.1 percent by 2022. This was even lower than the nonveteran rate of 3.6 percent (U.S. Bureau of Labor Statistics, 2023).[1]

More than a decade has passed since the height of the Great Recession, however, and the environment in which new nonprofit organizations were stood up with strong corporate buy-in has changed. The armed forces face new kinds of challenges in meeting recruiting goals, which could reduce the number of transitioning service members in coming years (Garamone, 2023). The philanthropic playing field has likely changed too. Some veteran advocates and organization leaders have become worried that securing funding will become more competitive in the coming years, and that organizations supporting veteran employment could find themselves scrambling hard for the resources they need. This kind of uncertainty has caused concern among veteran nonprofit leadership and advocates. More specifically, there is unease about the financial sustainability of nonprofit organizations dedicated to veteran employment in the coming years. At the same time, the federal government is increasingly relying on nonprofit organizations to support veteran employment through public-nonprofit partnerships, so ensuring the effectiveness and sustainability of these organizations is essential.

Researchers from the RAND Epstein Family Veterans Policy Research Institute examined the present and near-future landscape of nonprofit organizations focused on veteran employment. This report documents our research efforts and offers timely recommendations for nonprofit leaders and federal government policymakers to consider as they continue to commit themselves to veteran transition services. This work may also be of interest to veteran employment program designers and implementers, funders of such programs and initiatives, and anyone in need of a more accurate understanding of the landscape in which veteran services operate.

This report complements the report *Federal Programs to Assist Military-to-Civilian Employment Transitions*, which assesses federal military-to-civilian transition support pro-

[1] Because veterans differ from nonveterans in many ways, comparing unemployment rates across the two groups can be misleading. For example, veterans are younger and more likely to be male than the population as a whole. But a key difference is that *all* new veterans have recently gone through a job change (leaving the military); for this reason, they tend to experience a period of unemployment. See Loughran (2014) for a longer discussion of veteran unemployment and of the differences between veterans and nonveterans.

grams (Kleykamp et al., 2024). Together, these two reports map and assess the resources available to the veteran population. They also highlight collaborative opportunities that federal, nonprofit, and private organizations could consider to ensure the long-term sustainability of high-performing veteran employment support services.

The remainder of this introductory chapter offers a brief statement of our study methods, a closer look at veteran employment and unemployment, and a high-level overview of the role of nonprofits in the veteran space. Further details about our methods can be found in corresponding chapters and select appendixes.

In Brief: How This Study Was Conducted

To understand the current landscape of the veteran-serving employment-focused nonprofit community, our team sought to answer five key questions (see box).

Veteran-Serving Nonprofit Organizations: Research Questions

1. **Nonprofit resilience:** How do leaders in this community perceive the sustainability of their programs and services, particularly when it comes to future fundraising, and collaboration?
2. **Effectiveness:** How do veteran-serving nonprofits measure effectiveness? How can their measures be improved?
3. **Current financing:** What is the financial landscape of nonprofit organizations supporting veteran transition today, and how is it changing?
4. **Donation prospects:** What are the prospects for future charitable giving to veterans' causes?
5. **Federal agency collaboration:** How do veteran-serving nonprofits collaborate with government agencies, and what are the challenges with public-private partnerships?

Multiple data sources and analytic methods were used to answer these questions. Our team (1) held interviews with leaders from nonprofit organizations, (2) reviewed select organizations' annual reports to identify existing measures of effectiveness, (3) analyzed tax filings from the sector to assess trends through time, (4) conducted a national survey to collect individual opinions on philanthropic donations to veteran-serving organizations, and (5) reviewed the literature on public-private partnerships to identify types of partnerships and the challenges and opportunities associated with each. Each of these methods is described more fully in the corresponding chapters that address each question.

Veteran Unemployment: How Good or Bad Is It and for Whom?

This chapter started with somewhat of a good news story: Multiple policies and the efforts of different organizations had brought positive change about in the lives of post-9/11 veteran job seekers by 2022. Overall, research shows that when considered as a broad group, U.S. military veterans fare well when it comes to employment after service. In general, veterans have higher levels of education (Rolen, 2017) and household incomes and experience lower rates of poverty than nonveterans (Bennett, 2019).

Yet it is important to remember that not all groups of veterans fare equally well. Some subpopulations have worse outcomes on standard measures of economic success. For example, Black and Hispanic veterans have higher poverty and unemployment rates and lower household incomes than white veterans, though they outperform their nonveteran peers (Bennett, 2019). Women veterans, despite having higher educational attainment than their men counterparts, earn significantly less—though they earn substantially more than women who have not served (Tamborini and Purcell, 2023). Those who left the military as junior enlisted personnel are less likely than prior officers to already have a civilian job lined up (Parker et al., 2019). Finding a comparably well-paying civilian job is more difficult for those who served in some military jobs, such as infantry, in which fewer skills easily translate to civilian equivalents (McEntarfer, 2020). Veterans with disability ratings higher than 70 percent earn much less than other veterans and have significantly lower labor force participation rates (Congressional Budget Office, 2023). Younger veterans, particularly those ages 18 to 24, have significantly higher rates of unemployment than those who are older (Syracuse University, 2024).

Those who entered the military with a higher number of adverse childhood experiences and then experienced either sexual trauma or combat trauma during their military service are more likely to have financial problems, and high levels of physical and mental health conditions among these veterans (Perkins and Mogan, 2023) indicate that employment-focused solutions may be inadequate to solve their complex challenges. Efforts are underway to find methods of identifying veterans at higher risk of experiencing negative post-transition outcomes to facilitate targeted interventions (Stanley et al., 2022; Romaniuk et al., 2023).

Even among those who are gainfully employed, some evidence hints that they have not been able to unlock their full potential in the civilian sector (LinkedIn, 2023). As the veteran unemployment rate stabilized, concerns mounted that this was accomplished by pushing employment at any job, including those below veterans' skill and experience levels, rather than at fulfilling careers, potentially decreasing job satisfaction and increasing turnover. The military-civilian divide could hinder efforts to effectively match veterans with optimal civilian employment opportunities by making it more difficult to convey military experience, whether hard or soft skills, to civilian employers (Carter et al., 2017). However, lack of consensus on the meaning of the term *underemployment* complicates analyzing trends through time. The U.S. Bureau of Labor Statistics defines *underemployment* as those who work part time but would prefer to work full time, but others apply different definitions. Analysis conducted by the Call of Duty Endowment and ZipRecruiter found that employed veteran job seekers among their user base were more likely than their nonveteran counterparts to be underemployed, as calculated by comparing their skill level with the required skill level for their current job (Barrera and Carter, 2017). LinkedIn found that it takes its veteran members longer to reach senior positions, such as director or vice president (LinkedIn, 2023).

The Veterans Metrics Initiative, a longitudinal study of a cohort of post-9/11 veterans, found that 62 percent of respondents self-reported subjective underemployment based on their perceived leadership experience, skills, or education (Davenport et al., 2022).

Assessing the Role of Veteran-Serving Nonprofits in Employment

Taken together, the findings in the research discussed above indicate that it is too early to simply declare "mission accomplished" on veteran employment. The work being done by various public, private, and nonprofit partners to serve this population, collectively known as the *Sea of Goodwill* after a white paper by that name published by the Office of the Chairman of the Joint Chiefs of Staff (Chairman's Office of Reintegration, 2014), remains important to ensuring that those who volunteer to serve our nation against all enemies can thrive after service (Copeland and Sutherland, 2010). Nonprofit organizations have long played a significant role in supporting transitioning service members and veterans in a legacy extending back over a century for some member-based veterans service organizations (VSOs). In the post-9/11 era, additional organizations, some with a more explicit focus on employment and receiving more corporate funding, have also flourished. In fact, federal transition programming increasingly partners with these nongovernment organizations. For example, some federal programs help transitioning service members find employment by directly referring them to veteran employment–focused nongovernment organizations. However, now that large-scale U.S. involvement in conflicts abroad has ended and public attention has been captured by domestic crises, including the coronavirus disease 2019 (COVID-19) pandemic and racial injustice, some who serve and support veterans have expressed concerns about how to maintain the Sea of Goodwill and whether nonprofit organizations in it are positioned for long-term financial viability. Others have wondered whether all veteran employment–focused nonprofit organizations are equally effective and about the relationship between financial sustainability and effectiveness.

Previous work by the Center for a New American Security (CNAS) showed that, while revenue to the veteran-serving nonprofit sector broadly was increasing, growth was not distributed evenly among different types of organizations within the space. However, that work has not been updated in several years and, as discussed in more depth below, the CNAS methodology may not have fully captured trends among nonprofits serving veterans. Additionally, very little research has been done to examine the financial sustainability and effectiveness of the segment of the veteran-serving nonprofit ecosystem specifically dedicated to supporting transition and employment—even though some organizations have become formally integrated into federal government programming for transitioning servicemembers. This report was conceived to fill this gap.

How This Report Is Organized

This report is organized into several chapters, each of which explores the issues facing the veteran nonprofit ecosystem through a different lens. In Chapter 2, we give voice to leaders in the employment-focused veteran-serving nonprofit space to better understand their outlook on the future and how they measure success. Chapter 3 describes how nonprofit veteran employment organizations currently measure their effectiveness and presents a framework for standardizing and improving measurement to better compare across programs and organizations. In Chapter 4, we delve into trends in the finances of the veteran-serving nonprofit sector, both as a whole and focusing on those organizations that provide employment-focused services, also identifying challenges in conducting these analyses. Chapter 5 presents the findings of a nationally representative survey about individual charitable giving to veteran-serving nonprofits. Chapter 6 describes what types of collaborations exist between public and nonprofit organizations in other sectors with the goal of revealing whether there are underexploited avenues within the veteran space that could enhance future sustainability. In Chapter 7, we integrate the results into synthesized recommendations on how those who plan, implement, fund, and oversee programming to serve this population can build on past successes to institutionalize a sustainable future for high-performing services that support transitioning service members effectively.

Several appendixes present additional details and information about our methods and findings: Appendix A is a list of the organizations that participated in interviews; Appendix B outlines how interviews were coded; Appendix C summarizes additional findings from interviews with nonprofit organizations; Appendix D describes tools, such as a logic model, that organizations can use to assess their effectiveness; Appendixes E and F present information on how nonprofit organizations are categorized by the Internal Revenue Service; Appendix G summarizes additional survey findings; and finally, in Appendix H, we review the history and evolution of the U.S. Department of Veterans Affairs' (VA's) public-private partnerships.

CHAPTER 2

Views of Veteran-Serving Nonprofit Leaders

Meredith Kleykamp, Kayla M. Williams, Julia Vidal Verástegui, and Shaddy K. Saba

Nonprofit and nongovernment transition programs play a vital role in serving the comprehensive transition needs of veterans or transitioning service members and their spouses. But, like all nonprofits, these programs must stay alert and be agile to maintain the funding needed to deliver essential services, especially in constantly changing conditions. Program and organization leaders working in the field can offer valuable insight into the current functioning of the veteran transition ecosystem and about its possible future. Because of their experience and expertise, we interviewed leaders of 15 nonprofit organizations to help us address the first study question:

> **Research Question 1**
>
> **Nonprofit resilience.** How do leaders in this community perceive the sustainability of their programs and services, particularly when it comes to future fundraising and collaboration?

The insights garnered from the interviews provide context for other study data. Here, leaders discuss their concerns about their missions, ability to sustain their work into the future, and how their efforts align with current federal programs to support veteran transition.

Methods: Interviewee Selection, Interview Protocol, and Data Interpretation

Our study team developed a list of potential interviewees by soliciting opinions from key stakeholders active in veteran transition and employment. These stakeholders helped us to identify which organizations were seen as leaders, as well as which programs were especially effective. We also asked interviewees for additional recommendations of organizations to speak with and relied on our own expertise in the field to seek out those leaders and organizations that we knew would offer insightful input.

Not all organizations responded to our interview requests. The final sample of 15 leaders provided insights that ultimately reflect only those willing to participate. Notably, missing from our sample are organizations that traditionally serve people with disabilities, some of whom are veterans—though these organizations do not primarily serve veterans. Additionally, small or local organizations are likely underrepresented, since they would not have been mentioned as leaders in this area. The organizations represented in our interviews included those that (1) focus on veteran employment and transition, (2) would be considered VSOs, (3) fund other nonprofits serving veterans, and/or (4) focus on leadership development of veterans. The list of participating organizations that agreed to be recognized is presented in Appendix A.[1]

We were particularly interested in better understanding organization concerns about measuring effectiveness, future sustainability, perceptions of issue competition in philanthropy, and novel funding models to sustain veteran programming. Interviews were conducted using a common protocol that ensured specific topics were covered in the discussion but that also allowed for a free-flowing conversation and new ideas untapped by the protocol questions. Interviews were recorded by a notetaker (they were not audio recorded and transcribed), and any quotations reflect quotations from the notes and may not reflect a direct quotation from an interview participant unless noted as such. We generally followed the "flexible coding" approach advocated and described by Deterding and Waters (2021). Flexible coding offers an alternative framework to the grounded theory approach. In particular, the approach embraces qualitative interview research that is not intended to be purely inductive but rather is grounded in what is already known from prior theory or empirical studies and is conducted using software to facilitate analysis. Often, the process involves large samples, multiple qualitative data sources, and a team of coders and analysts. A key step in the flexible coding approach is indexing the interview transcript to the interview protocol, which is then followed by developing and applying analytic codes specific to a particular research question that integrate emergent insights with what is known from the literature.

Our semistructured interview protocol was organized to ask about several different topics, which were used as top-level index codes. A team member coded interview notes from the 14 interviews using codes derived from the interview protocol, as suggested by the flexible coding approach, to link large chunks of text to major theoretical or conceptual ideas meant to be captured by the interview protocol. This allows for later review of text around a common topic. We also identified additional codes that reflected the preliminary insights gained by interviewers during their conversations with these representatives and with each other as the study progressed. Appendix B presents the codes used. We do not analyze the

[1] We conducted 15 interviews, and 14 organizations agreed to be listed by name in the report. The 15th interview was conducted after coding was complete, so data from that interview were not incorporated into the analysis.

coding quantitatively, in part because of the small and unrepresentative sample of interviewed organizations. Rather, we use the codes to organize broad themes from the interviews and to identify relevant examples of shared themes. Although we do not analyze the coded data quantitatively, we do rely on prevalence of a particular perspective or theme as a guide for identifying it as important to discuss. But we do not use prevalence further to suggest that one theme is more or less important than another based on prevalence, given the small and nonrepresentative sample we interviewed.

Major Themes from Nonprofit Organization Representatives

Organizations Provide Individualized Employment Services to Diverse Veteran Clients

The organizations whose representatives we interviewed were diverse in their mission and characteristics. Seven organizations (or dedicated programs within larger organizations) centered their efforts on employment and transition services, three were VSOs whose work includes employment and transition, two were funders, and three were organizations or programs that had a leadership focus, as well as providing employment and transition support. When asked about the work of their organizations, representatives identified different groups of veterans they primarily served. Some of the very large national programs served a near universal population of veterans and spouses "from the grassroots and grass tops," as one representative described.

Some organizations specifically noted their interest in working to serve underrepresented or at-risk veteran populations. Groups of particular interest included women veterans, junior enlisted veterans, or racial minority veterans. Some organizations described whom they serve based not on the characteristics of their clients, but instead on the problems or challenges they were facing. Issues were underemployment, mental health, food security, workforce readiness, and health and fertility challenges.

Half of the organizations interviewed were chosen because of their focus on employment. Thus, naturally, employment and transition to the civilian workforce were noted as major challenges by these organizations. These employment-focused organizations noted challenges beyond simply "unemployment": underemployment, licensure and certifications, résumé development, and focused training on employer-desirable skills were discussed in particular. While such organizations may have once simply hosted job fairs and job boards, they are now doing individualized, one-on-one work—with transitioning service members, veterans, and spouses—for which they are not receiving funds from DoD or other federal transition programs.

Federal Programs Are Necessary but Not Sufficient, and There Is Limited Federal Funding for Nongovernment Transition Programs

We asked organizations about their relationship with federal transition programs and services to better understand the overlap in services, or gaps and needs unmet by federal programs. We also discussed the organizations' perspectives on the current state of federal transition programs and whether they felt federal programs were successful. For some organization representatives, this meant discussing TAP, which is the near-mandatory program to help transitioning service members understand their benefits from VA and the U.S. Department of Labor (DoL) and how to begin to develop a résumé and job search strategy (see Appendix C for these perspectives).[2] While some expressed critical views of the federal approach to transition services and programs, others had more-nuanced views about the limits of federal obligation to transition outcomes. A few representatives discussed the kinds of services that federal programs are not focusing on—namely, the cultural and identity-related questions and challenges that can occur when transitioning out of the military.

Some representatives voiced a desire for the federal government to provide funding to nonprofit organizations to do more of the work to provide transition assistance. One person noted that the federal government might be better suited to "invest in others, rather than design and run their own programs." This person commented that while "businesses need to meet [the] demands of customers to survive, government programs have to be more limited in how they can design programs and evolve."

From the perspective of these leaders, the veteran transition experience would be better addressed if the federal government provided the funds to others to implement programs and demonstrate their effectiveness. That did not mean eliminating federal programs entirely. Rather, it referred to the development of a much more mature model that relied on public-private partnerships to help veterans transition, especially into civilian employment. (In Chapter 6, we discuss various types of collaborations between government and nonprofit organizations that could serve as models to pursue.)

Financial Sustainability of Nonprofit Transition Programs

Some interviewees had ongoing concerns about their financial sustainability. Others felt fairly confident in the stability and sustainability of their funding streams. While all organizations understood that securing sustainable funding was an ongoing component of their work, the extent to which organizations felt extreme financial pressures was varied among this group of organizations that are relatively large, well-functioning, and respected in the

---

2 More than 90 percent of transitioning service members participated in the core three-day TAP classes between April 1, 2021, and March 31, 2022, according to a GAO study. In that same time frame, 56 percent of transitioning service members attended one of the two-day tracks (employment, education, or entrepreneurship), for which attendance is mandatory across all branches only for those "deemed to require maximum transition support" (GAO, 2022).

space. It may be the case that smaller organizations might feel more existential financial pressures to sustain their programs.

Some interviewees expressed concerns about sustainability in light of increased referrals from federal government programs, worrying that they cannot serve more veterans without government funding. One representative noted this concern, reflecting on a meeting with DoL officials about a federal program that refers veterans to nonprofit organizations:

> Had a meeting with DoL leaders wanting the partners to tell the story of successes, and an organization said, "But we need a serious conversation about support—will we be contracted to provide it? Will there be appropriations? How are WE going to be able to continue to support it?" The conversation didn't progress past that. DoL said their budget priorities were to add more sites and add more [program] counselors and left it at that.

For almost all nonprofit organizations, how to sustain financial viability is a major and ongoing concern. The organizations represented by the leaders we interviewed largely rely on philanthropy to sustain their programs. Thus, they are very aware that their programs rely on the goodwill of the public, large corporate funders, or foundation grantors, and less on contracts or grants from the government.

In the discussion of finances and financial sustainability, the following themes emerged:

- **Competition among veteran-serving organizations:** Most organizations understood the competitive landscape of other veteran-serving programs and articulated a general hierarchy of a handful of large, prominent organizations combined with many smaller and more niche organizations that serve a narrow client base or focus on a very specific activity. Most saw the competition among organizations as healthy competition, forcing organizations to perform well and to be accountable by demonstrating positive outcomes and program effectiveness to remain viable. The shared sense of there being only a handful of organizations that were real leaders in the space, especially around veteran employment, led some representatives to speculate that smaller "mom and pop" organizations might be consolidated or eliminated. One representative felt that "only about 20 or so organizations are real competitors." Another representative from a prominent program said their organization "partners with organizations that may be seen as competitors. Vetting criteria is that they must have national impact. Smaller, local organizations are not likely to meet that even if they have a good mission."
- **Issue competition:** The organizational leaders we spoke with felt current and anticipated future funding pressures caused by shifting philanthropic trends—in particular, the rise of interest in social justice issues. Some representatives shared concerns that funding was in decline for veterans' issues, mentioning past high-profile corporate donors who were shifting their philanthropy to other causes. One interviewee noted,

    > We're very reliant on corporate partners, which is very hard since they are not multi-year and they are drying up post-Afghanistan. Our [redacted] grant is dropping to

> 25 percent of what they used to give and this is the last year. When [corporations] close their veterans pillar or move away from something they've done for years, that's hard. It's hard to talk about this with peers but I think there is some anxiety.

Another reported,

> This year, we have had companies that have funded us for years now say no more, or reduce, but also some coming on. . . . But there is more focus on programs other than veterans now among funders . . . movement to economically challenged, food insecurity, disadvantaged in general as a shift in funder interest or priorities.

The changing trends in corporate social responsibility in terms of salient issues affects how veteran-serving organizations position and market themselves and their programs.

- **Government role in funding veteran-serving programs and organizations.** Nonprofit organizations may receive funding from multiple sources: small individual donations, corporate or foundation philanthropy, membership dues in some cases, and government grants and contracts. The representatives we spoke with had differing levels of reliance on and experience with government sources of funding. Some held relatively strong views that their programs should remain outside government, seeing employment programs as a responsibility of corporate America to support. Other programs found that the bureaucratic and reporting requirements to receive government grants and contracts were very burdensome, especially for leaner organizations without the staff or overhead to manage those requirements. One representative noted that

> [Government funding] should look like grants. . . . DoD doesn't like grants, but for nonprofits, federal contracts create reporting requirements that are challenging for small organizations. . . . Needs a different operating structure internally to manage federal grants versus contracts.

While some organizations were successfully managing to secure government grants and contracts and had the staffing to manage the reporting and other requirements that come with government funds, other organizations, large and small, were experimenting with novel means of funding their operations. These included providing services to nonveteran or military clients and using the proceeds to fund veteran programs, selling software or other internally developed program management tools to other organizations, and leveraging the vast amount of data being collected on program participants.

Conclusion

Taken together, these interviews with organization representatives suggest that nonprofit programs provide important services for transitioning service members, veterans, and their families. Such organizations are a crucial component of the broader ecosystem that aids in transition, particularly employment transitions. These organizations work to meet needs unmet by federal programs, such as TAP, by providing more individualized or specialized services than the TAP program can offer. They also receive referrals from federal partners through formal and informal mechanisms. But importantly, these employment- and leadership-focused nonprofits do not receive a great deal of funding, if any, from the federal government to provide these services. Most organizations rely on philanthropy, mixing sources from private individual, corporate, and/or family and foundation giving. The interviewees we spoke with expressed a growing concern about their ability to sustain key transition programming in the face of possible issue competition for charitable giving. Many others expressed a concern about financial sustainability at a time when the federal government was planning to increase its demands on these programs. For those organizations, there were serious concerns about their ability to sustain current levels, much less reach even greater levels, of service provision without some financial contribution from the federal government.

Organization leaders also talked in interviews about how the standards for demonstrating effectiveness of federal transition programs were lacking or nonexistent. Many felt that because they had to demonstrate their programs' value to continue to receive funds from donors, they were better positioned to know what specific approaches worked in improving veterans' transition outcomes. While few of the organizations implemented best-in-class program evaluation techniques, all reported output metrics, including participant outcome data to demonstrate the value of their programs to veterans and their families. We turn to this discussion next.

CHAPTER 3

Measuring Program Effectiveness

Jennie W. Wenger and Julia Vidal Verástegui

In this chapter, we consider how program effectiveness is measured or assessed in the veteran transition ecosystem and how these measures can be improved. In short, beyond program inputs and outputs, there is little consistent measurement of program outcomes and impacts.[1] Some funders, including the federal government, may make the argument that resources should be dedicated to nonprofit organizations that are high-performing and can demonstrate effectiveness at improving veteran employment outcomes. Minimally effective or even ineffective programs waste resources, potentially siphoning them from more-effective programs that could use resources more effectively and efficiently. Ineffective programs may disappoint veterans who do not see desired results and lead them to perceive that the system failed them. Veterans have limited data to use in making choices when seeking assistance and, ultimately, pay the price when using ineffective programs that do not facilitate quick and successful transitions to work.

Research Question 2

Effectiveness. How do veteran-serving nonprofits measure effectiveness? How can their measures be improved?

Determining which organizations are effective requires standardized and comparable measures of effectiveness, with shared definitions of the outcomes of interest. In this chapter, we report on the specific metrics used by veteran-serving nonprofit organizations based on interviews with leaders and annual reporting. We rely on data from a scan of annual reports

[1] *Inputs* and *outputs* typically capture a program's resources and expected immediate results, respectively. *Outcome measures* focus on the changes that are expected to occur as a result of the program. See Appendix D for more information.

from a selected group of nonprofits and from interviews with leaders of several organizations that serve transitioning service members and veterans. We also lay out a framework describing the types of measures that are needed across nonprofit organizations that serve veterans.

Current State of Measuring Effectiveness of Nonprofit Veteran Employment Organizations

In our interviews with nonprofit leaders, many noted the demand for transparency and metrics for accountability in the nonprofit veteran program ecosystem. To continue to receive funding, particularly from foundations or corporations, these organizations must show evidence of program effectiveness. As one person noted, "We have doubled in size over the last five years because of early focus on outcomes. Donors demanded a great deal of accountability, focused on data and metrics that mattered to them." Some representatives also felt that lack of program evaluation or other metrics for effectiveness across the space had the potential to water down willingness to support veteran-serving nonprofits. Several leaders made similar points that the presence of programs that do not engage in best practices of evaluation and reporting potentially siphons resources from those with demonstrated effectiveness and, potentially, harms the space overall, as it competes against other concerns seeking individual, corporate, and foundation giving.

However, there do not seem to be widely accepted, consistent measures of program outcomes or effectiveness used across the different organizations, despite longstanding calls for such efforts (see, for example, Berglass and Harrell, 2012).

Metrics Used by Nonprofit Veteran Employment Organizations in Annual Reports

Programs often published their evaluation outcomes and other program metrics in their annual reports or websites, allowing the public and other stakeholders to see how well they are serving veterans, how resources are being used to effect desired goals, and who is being served by their programs. To supplement the explanations interviewees provided about the metrics they use, we reviewed public reports from several prominent organizations to ascertain the specific data points and metrics that were being collected and reported. Table 3.1 provides specific examples of key information included in public reports from 11 organizations seen as active in the employment sector of the veteran-serving nonprofit space. We recorded what types of inputs, outputs, and outcomes they reported, particularly related to employment-related services, as well as additional information about what types of metrics or data are collected. This overview does not capture all metrics reported by all veteran-serving nonprofits that provide any employment-related services. However, by showcasing the array of data reported by this subset of organizations, we highlight the challenges of attempting to compare effectiveness between organizations.

TABLE 3.1

Comparisons of Program Effectiveness Are Not Possible Because Organizations Report Different Metrics

Organization	Example Reported Metrics	Types of Information Reported in Annual Reports
American Corporate Partners (ACP)	• 98% satisfaction from protégés • 34,000+ veterans and active-duty spouses have become ACP Alumni since 2010 • 4,465 veterans and active-duty spouses completed the mentoring program in 2023	• $90,000+: ACP's estimate of the average salary for protégés who obtained a job during their mentorship • 2,682 protégés obtained meaningful employment during their mentorships in 2023 • Protégés obtained employment at 1,159 companies • 85% of ACP protégés who obtained employment in 2021 remained at the same company for at least one year • Breakdown of protégé demographics by military branch, officer versus enlisted, gender, active-duty spouses, ethnicity, education level • Results of veteran and military spouse protégés' survey results and mentors' survey results
Disabled American Veterans (DAV)	• 101 career fairs in 2023 with 31,723 attendees, resulting in more than 12,590 job offers • More than 3 million volunteer hours in VA facilities and communities, 9.2+ million miles, and nearly 246,000 rides for veterans to their medical appointments	• Annual reports provide number of claims processed, the number of benefits advocates nationwide (3,610 in 2023), 209,000 new claims, and 303,481 claimants counseled • Transition services: More than 45,000 service members assisted • 66 resolutions included in legislation introduced, and 7 DAV resolutions enacted into law
ETS Sponsorship	• No list of metrics, but the "Program Overview" document has a list of outcomes for the program	• No actual metrics listed, but a list of metrics that executives intend to use to measure the effectiveness of the program: employment outcomes, education outcomes, health care outcomes, referral outcomes, self-referral outcomes, and program outcomes • The document also states that some of these metrics are not yet being collected because they need to be baselined over multiple iterations of the program

Table 3.1—Continued

Organization	Example Reported Metrics	Types of Information Reported in Annual Reports
FourBlock	• Typical cohort is ~75% former enlisted and ~25% former officers • 4,500+ veterans have graduated from the program • 500+ companies have hired FourBlock alumni • $100,837 average alumni starting salary, full-time, self-reported as of 2023	• As of the 2022 annual report, 608 veterans and 41 military spouses were served • From a 2022 alumni follow-up survey, 87% of 2022 alumni found new careers within 6 months of program completion (FourBlock Foundation, undated) • 57% of veterans stay at their first job more than 12 months (national average)
Hire Heroes USA	• 100,000+ confirmed hires (total to date) • 36,000+ jobs on the board • 1,450+ volunteers (Hire Heroes USA, undated)	• "Hire Heroes Report" divided into 3 parts (Hire Heroes USA, undated): intake, helped, and hired, to represent client life cycle • Internal Data Operations team that conducts analysis on the job seekers • Metrics in 2022 report: individual client records, total registered, total helped, total helped that registered in 2022, confirmed hires, confirmed hires (first time), and confirmed hires (multiples) (Hire Heroes USA, 2022)
HOH	• 74% of virtual hiring fair attendees in 2020 moved to the next step • 617,000+ hires through HOH events and programs • HOH's 2019 in-person hiring events saw an offer rate of 43% (HOH, 2023)	• "Military Spouse Employment Flash Survey" to track emerging trends in military spouse employment outcomes • Report on the "Hidden Financial Costs of Military Spouse Unemployment"
Onward to Opportunity (O2O)	• Participants are twice as likely to leave jobs for better opportunities at the 6-month mark • O2O participants receive a starting salary an average of $7,000 higher than nonparticipants • On average, O2O participants receive a $13,000 higher salary for E-6 paygrade and below	• To evaluate the success of the program, O2O conducted a study comparing it with a matched group from The Veterans Metrics Initiative (TVMI) • Major outcomes evaluated were starting salary and leaving a job for a better opportunity (job retention)
The American Legion	• Veteran employment: 3,060 job training programs; 1,019 posts in career fairs; and 2,251 veterans placed in jobs (2022) (American Legion undated)	• 606 veterans registered for three nationally sponsored American Legion career events in 2023 • Member of Task Force Movement, which aims to place veterans and their spouses in industries in need (e.g., trucking)

Table 3.1—Continued

Organization	Example Reported Metrics	Types of Information Reported in Annual Reports
United States Veterans Initiative (U.S. VETS)	• 12,573 veterans served in 2022 • 1,418 job placements • 53,846 supportive counseling sessions	• 2,202 veterans served by workforce programs (2023) • 1,418 job placements (2023) • 250 employer partners (2023) • 140 veterans trained as peer specialists (2023)
VetJobs	• 100,000+ service members, veterans, and their families placed since 2010 • 200,000+ military-affiliated individuals provided training and career development services since 2010	• $73,000 average salary for military and veterans placed (2023) • 8,942 transitioning military, National Guard, Reserves, and veterans placed into meaningful careers (2023) • 42,000+ training courses completed (2023) • 700–1,000 new registrations a week (2023)
Wounded Warrior Project (WWP)	• In FY 2023, WWP invested nearly $260 million in life-changing programs for warriors, family members, and caregivers	• Financial wellness: 63,800+ career coaching services provided, 1,500+ warrior and family members achieving employment (2023) • WWP surveys warriors that it serves regarding their needs and lists the following impacts in its 2023 annual report: – Connection: 4,400+ virtual and in-person events; 96% said that they feel socially connected to their peers after participating in WWP events – Mental health and wellness: 70% experienced fewer posttraumatic stress disorder symptoms after care through the Warrior Care Network and 66,300+ hours of treatment provided – Physical health and wellness: 45% experienced a reduction in pain, and 51% experienced an improvement in sleep quality.

SOURCES: HOH, 2023; ACP, undated; FourBlock, undated; FourBlock Foundation, undated; Hire Heroes USA, undated; Hire Heroes USA, 2022; WWP, 2024; U.S. Vets, undated; American Legion, undated; ETS Sponsorship, 2021; Syracuse University, undated-a; VetJobs, 2024.

From this selection of organizations and their public reports, it is clear that programs may report a wide variety of measures (inputs, outputs, or outcomes), including the following:

- number of program participants, including number of service member, veteran, and/or military spouse participants and/or number of employers or jobs in a job board or fair
- satisfaction with program
- number completing program
- money spent on program
- number of hires made
- number of hires remaining in same position after 12 months
- average starting salary.

In addition to these frequently reported metrics, particularly employment-related metrics, some organizations with broader missions may report others:

- number of disability compensation claims processed (for organizations assisting with wounded or disabled veterans)
- dollar amounts given or hours of assistance services provided
- volunteer hours provided in serving veterans
- social media impressions
- number of veterans provided with stable housing
- dollar amount of VA benefits organization helped secure for veterans
- outcomes of political advocacy actions.

Some programs also report on the demographics of their program participants, and some offer a variety of financial information in their annual reports as well. Such information is crucial in understanding program impact, given the diversity among new veterans, who range from single-term young enlisted to 30-year retired officers. Since employment outcomes are shaped by prior military experience, occupational training and skills, educational attainment, and military-connected injury or illness, program outcomes will be affected by who participates in these programs.

Data are collected from program administrative data and from surveys of program participants. Few indicate using more-formal program evaluation methods, such as random assignment to various programs, comparisons with matched nonparticipants, or pre-/post-treatment designs. Many of the metrics reported reflect program inputs, activities, and/or outputs rather than outcomes; for example, programs may measure participation and satisfaction versus the number who secure a job or the average starting salary. And those programs that report outcome measures tend to report simple and straightforward measures, such as number placed in jobs. (There are exceptions; some programs report more-nuanced measures.)

The general pattern of information reported is not unexpected. Inputs, activities, and outputs can be measured during the program, while outcomes generally must be measured after the completion of the program (and thus require maintaining contact with former participants). For this practical reason, many programs typically report such measures as the number of participants, number and types of activities undertaken, and perhaps a few short-term outcomes, especially those that might be known by the end of the program. Additionally, programs often collect qualitative data on participant satisfaction. While this metric is not often used in formal program evaluation, such information is generally quite valuable to programs because it provides suggestions for program adjustment and improvement relatively quickly.

Next, we provide a framework for identifying and standardizing metrics across veteran-serving programs in this space, as well as some specific metrics used by a large federally funded program.

Framework for Identifying and Standardizing Metrics

While developing and defining a specific and exhaustive list of metrics to evaluate programs designed to support transitioning service members and veterans seeking employment is beyond the scope of this report, we do suggest several guidelines:

- Programs should seek to measure effectiveness, with an approach that attempts to document not only the number served and types of services provided but also the outcomes experienced by program participants.
- Programs should use a clear logic model (or, at a minimum, a theory of change) to express the expected outcomes and how services provided are linked to those outcomes. Appendix D provides a useful description and example of a logic model.
- Programs should include measures that assess multiple steps in the process and account for the diverse set of individuals using these programs (e.g., number of program participants, characteristics of program participants) as well as outcomes (e.g., employment status at 6, 12, and 24 months after program completion by type of program participant, mean and median salary of program participants by type).
- Benchmarks (from external sources) may be helpful to programs seeking to measure impact. Benchmarks may be especially appropriate for programs that serve participants facing substantial hurdles.
- To incorporate diverse perspectives on this complicated issue and maximize buy-in, consensus should be reached on what measures to include and how to define them by first seeking input from a variety of stakeholders and then publishing proposed measures to transparently solicit public comment.
- Once metrics have been identified and defined, federal agencies, including DoL, DoD, and VA, that work with and/or give grants to employment-focused veteran-serving nonprofits should require them to report on these metrics in a standardized and publicly available way to increase transparency and accountability.

- Foundations can support implementation by requiring grantees that do not partner with federal agencies to report on the same metrics.

The metrics adopted as part of the Workforce Innovation Opportunity Act (WIOA) serve as a potentially useful model for veteran-serving employment programs. WIOA exists to improve alignment between workforce development programs. Such programs seek to provide increased opportunities for employment, education, and training with the ultimate goal of improving the prosperity of individuals and communities (Pub. L. 113-128, 2014). Similar to veteran-serving employment programs, these programs serve many individuals with different strengths and challenges.[2] Job Corps is a large, long-established, federally funded program that seeks to develop skills among young people and assist in their search for employment. Job Corps, which operates more than 130 sites around the United States, is one of the many programs funded through WIOA.

The DoL requires that WIOA-funded programs report a common set of metrics or measures. These include the following:

- employment rates in the second and fourth quarter after program completion
- percentage of participants who are employed by the same employer in the second and fourth quarter after exit (retention)
- median earnings in the second quarter after program completion
- credential attainment within 12 months of program completion
- demonstration of skills gain.

Programs may also be required to report additional information. For example, Job Corps sites report ten additional measures; these include aspects of the following:

- program completion and dropout rates
- speed of job placement
- average starting salary
- enlistment in the Armed Services
- enrollment in apprenticeship programs
- rate of full-time employment.

This framework captures richer information than is typically collected by veteran-serving programs. While this exact framework may not be appropriate for most veteran-serving programs, adopting a common set of metrics for all programs and encouraging programs to collect additional information that reflects their specific activities or goals is a useful structure for veteran-serving employment programs.

---

[2] For a description of WIOA and the individual programs, see DoL, Employment and Training Administration, undated.

Another potential model is found in the work of Call of Duty Endowment; this group focuses on serving veterans by providing grants to a select group of organizations with a mission to place veterans in jobs. Call of Duty Endowment has developed a set of performance standards or metrics; organizations that receive grants are required to report a specific set of metrics on a quarterly basis. These include cost per placement, average starting salary, retention in the job at the 6- and 12-month points, and full- versus part-time placements (Call of Duty Endowment, undated).[3] This list has some overlap with the metrics that veteran-serving nonprofits report using in Table 3.1 and with the WIOA metrics discussed above. Call of Duty Endowment's list of metrics could serve as a starting point for the development of a set of appropriate, consistent metrics. Finally, Call of Duty Endowment awards a Seal of Distinction to recognize highly effective nonprofit veteran-serving organizations. This, too, could serve as a model for encouraging a wider array of veteran-serving organizations to report consistent data and to focus on effectiveness.

Conclusion

All organizations interviewed collect and report data of some kind and consider this an important way to demonstrate the value of their programs; however, inconsistencies in measures complicate comparisons across organizations. Data are typically collected from program administrative data and from surveys of program participants; few programs indicate using more-formal program evaluation methods, such as random assignment to various programs, comparisons with matched nonparticipants, or pre-/post-treatment designs. Many of the metrics used reflect program inputs and/or outputs rather than outcomes—for example, measuring participation and satisfaction versus securing a job, starting salary, or other characteristics of the job. Thus, programs often stop short of directly measuring information that allows conclusions about the programs' impacts.

Currently, there are no incentives in place to encourage organizations to transparently report on a consistent set of metrics. This hinders the ability of both veterans in need of high-quality services and potential funders seeking to support effective programs to identify which are high performing. While there is no single, appropriate metric for all veteran-serving programs, examples do exist, both in the veteran-serving space and in the broader job placement space; we discuss a couple of these. Of course, the choice of exactly which metrics to use is a serious one and should be made through a deliberate process that considers the exact services provided and involves numerous stakeholders. That said, there appears to be a role for funders to influence the types and quality of metrics used and reported. Such a

[3] The organization's website implies that other performance standards beyond the four listed above are used, but there is no readily available information to determine the details of any other performance standards.

change has the potential to improve the effectiveness of veteran-serving programs and, thus, result in better outcomes for transitioning veterans.

CHAPTER 4

Veteran-Serving Nonprofit Finances

Shaddy K. Saba and Kayla M. Williams

As noted in Chapter 2, many nonprofit organizations focused on veteran employment are concerned about the financial sustainability of their organizations. One way to assess whether these concerns are warranted is to examine the tax records of the veteran nonprofit sector. While this does not provide insight into the financial well-being of any individual organization, and—as we note below—there are limitations to this approach, it does provide a high-level indicator of how the sector as a whole is faring.

Research Question 3

Current financing. What is the financial landscape of nonprofit organizations supporting veteran transition today, and how is it changing?

In the past decade, several reports have asked questions like this one (all authored by investigators at CNAS and not focused only on veteran transition). The first, *Charting the Sea of Goodwill*, profiled nonprofit organizations serving veterans and reported that, while in 2014 their revenue appeared relatively flat for over a decade, demand for services was increasing, suggesting a need for novel funding streams and business models in the sector (Kuzminski and Carter, 2015). The second, *Changing Tides in the Sea of Goodwill*, revealed that, while large post-9/11 organizations had experienced the largest income growth in the sector between 2007 and 2015, large *pre*-9/11 organizations (i.e., traditional VSOs) still dominated the sector in terms of their total income and assets (McCormick, Moore, and Swick, 2018). Finally, *Funding Flows in the Sea of Goodwill* identified the major funders in the veteran philanthropy space in 2019 and the types of services they fund (Moore et al., 2019). This chapter should be thought of as an update to these reports as we review the financial landscape of veteran-serving nonprofits using the most-current available data. However, we also found that mechanisms available to monitor these trends face limitations. For example, organizations that provide services to veterans are classified by the Internal Revenue Service (IRS) under a variety of activity codes. Our approach examines organizations using a specific activity code (W30, military and veterans organizations), meaning this method likely underestimates the amount of support available to this population.

Financial Data and Analytic Methods

The current analysis of the financial landscape of veteran-serving nonprofits uses data included in nonprofits' organizational tax filings. These were reported to the IRS using one of several 990 forms based on their organizational characteristics and revenue (IRS, 2023a). Tax returns of nonprofit organizations are made publicly available by law as a condition of receiving tax-exempt status, and information from tax returns is available in raw form from the IRS or in processed form from several data centers (IRS, 2023b). Following the methodology used by CNAS in prior reports on the veteran-serving nonprofit sector, we obtained data for our analyses from the GuideStar database of U.S. nonprofit organizations (Candid, undated).

We included in the present analyses organizations that were classified under the National Taxonomy of Exempt Entities (NTEE) code W30, because such organizations are "military and veterans' organizations" within the larger category of "public and societal benefit" organizations (see Appendix E for a list of all NTEE codes). Since there are tens of thousands of organizations registered with the NTEE code W30, to manage the scope of our analysis, we limited the data pull to organizations reporting at least $1 in revenue during their most recent tax filing year, resulting in a dataset of just under 7,400 organizations. We next excluded financial services organizations, including mutual aid associations (e.g., Navy Mutual Aid Association) and providers of insurance and other financial services (e.g., Consumer Credit Counseling Services, Virginia National Guard Ventures), both to be in alignment with the CNAS methodology and because these organizations' data distorted revenue information for the dataset. These steps resulted in a dataset of 7,366 nonprofit, W30 organizations. Of these, we characterized 107 as employment-related or job training organizations by filtering for GuideStar taxonomy subject codes "Employment" and "Job training" and searching for relevant keywords in organizations' mission statements.

As noted above, this method is an imperfect way of identifying nonprofit organizations that provide services and support to transitioning service members and veterans, likely underestimating the size of the "sea of goodwill" (see Appendix F for further discussion of this limitation). However, replicating the CNAS method to the maximum extent possible enables monitoring trends in the revenue of W30-coded organizations through time.

During the COVID-19 pandemic, IRS 990 data releases were significantly delayed. However, in May 2023, the IRS released around one million 990s, which were rapidly available through GuideStar (Ward and Clerkin, 2023). Our analyses of funding flows (i.e., total revenue and expenses reported on 990s) within the veteran-serving nonprofit sector included only those organizations with tax filings in 2020 or later (approximately 80 percent of organizations). Roughly three-quarters of most-recent tax filings available for analysis were from 2021 and 2022.

This dataset enabled us to assess trends in charitable giving to these W30 organizations. We were also able to explore challenges in using the W30 designation to analyze the sector of philanthropy dedicated to supporting veterans.

Trends in Philanthropy

Veteran-serving nonprofits are part of a larger philanthropic ecosystem. It is worth considering trends in giving more broadly before zooming in to assess trends in this segment of charitable giving. According to the Giving USA Foundation's 2023 annual report, total giving in 2022 was nearly $500 billion (Lilly Family School of Philanthropy, 2023b). This is a decline of more than 10 percent in constant dollars from 2021 in the wake of challenging economic conditions that affected the stock market, personal income, and inflation. This drop followed the two best years on record for nonprofit giving and affected nearly all categories of nonprofits. Giving to religion; human services; education; health; public-society benefit; arts, culture, and humanities; and environmental and animal organizations all declined in constant dollars, with only foundations and international affairs seeing growth over 2021 amounts.

In 2022, individual donations made up 64 percent of all charitable giving, followed by foundations at 21 percent, bequests at 9 percent, and corporations at 6 percent (Gaumer, 2023). DealAid (McCabe, 2023) summary statistics indicate that 56 percent of Americans donated to charity at least once in the previous year, and giving rates rise with age (less than one-third of Generation Z gives to charity, compared with about 60 percent of Millennials and Generation X, nearly 3 in 4 Baby Boomers, and 88 percent of the Silent Generation).

Affluent households are significantly more likely to donate to charity, and (not surprisingly) donate larger amounts. A 2023 Bank of America/Lilly Family School of Philanthropy study found that, of the 85 percent of affluent households that gave to charity in 2022, more than half reported that their giving is linked to issues they care most about, such as those in which they take interest or those that align with their personal values or beliefs (Lilly Family School of Philanthropy, 2023a; Bank of America, 2023). Among affluent individuals born prior to 1981, nearly 13 percent selected veterans' affairs as among the causes that matter most to them, compared with only 3.4 percent of subsequent generations, who were dramatically more likely to select climate change and education (Bank of America, 2023). These trends may bode ill for veteran organizations moving forward, given that far fewer individuals overall have a personal connection to the military in the era of the All-Volunteer Force. This issue is perhaps exacerbated among younger affluent charitable donors, given that the wealthy are less likely to serve in the military (Center for Naval Analyses, 2021) and that most Americans stay in the social class into which they are born (Urahn et al., 2012).

Funding Flows in the Veteran-Serving Nonprofit Sector

As it was infeasible to obtain yearly data for every organization included in the dataset, we examined revenue and change in revenue over the period from 2016 to 2022 for several subgroups of organizations. These included (1) the ten current highest-revenue W30 organizations coded as employment-related; (2) the ten current largest W30 organizations overall; (3) the ten largest organizations at the time of the 2019 CNAS report, for comparison through time since that publication (Moore et al., 2019); and (4) the headquarters of the traditional "Big Six" VSOs (The American Legion, American Veterans, DAV, Paralyzed Veterans of America [PVA], Veterans of Foreign Wars of the United States [VFW], and Vietnam Veterans of America).[1]

Although this report is primarily interested in understanding financial trends for employment-focused veteran-serving nonprofits, these analyses both contextualize their financial performance relative to related organizations and show trends through time for the broader W30 sector. The total revenue (which includes contributions and grants, program service revenue, investment income, and other revenue) for all W30 organizations in our data set was $4.28 billion.

The total revenue of the ten largest W30 organizations by revenue in 2022, shown in Table 4.1, is $1.50 billion, which is 35 percent of the $4.28 billion in total revenue of all W30 organizations.

As mentioned above, we sought to identify which W30 organizations focus on employment by filtering for GuideStar taxonomy subject codes "Employment" and "Job training" and searching for relevant keywords in organizations' mission statements. The revenue for the ten largest of those organizations is shown in Table 4.2. The goal of identifying these organizations was to assess approximately what percentage of the overall W30 sector is dedicated to employment support for transitioning service members and veterans, the focus of this study. However, this method did not identify organizations seen by our interviewees as playing the most significant role in employment services for transitioning service members and veterans (many of which do not use the W30 code, as discussed below), and none of the organizations listed in Table 4.2 has an exclusive focus on veteran employment.

To consider changes in revenue for these organizations over time, we selected the ten largest W30 organizations by revenue from the 2019 CNAS report and compared the revenue reported for each in 2016 and 2022 (in constant 2022 dollars). We identified some changes in the organizations that are generating the most revenue within the sector today (shown in Table 4.3): Three are no longer in the top ten in 2022. The total revenue for these ten organizations grew from $1 billion to $1.22 billion, an increase of 22 percent. For comparison, total charitable giving during that same time frame grew from $463 billion

[1] This likely represents an underestimation of the total size of the traditional VSOs, which often also have associated chapters, auxiliaries, and foundations. Each of these is incorporated as a separate legal entity and files separately; chapters may fall below the threshold of having to file a 990.

TABLE 4.1

2022 Revenue and Expenses of Top Ten W30 Organizations (by Revenue)

Organization	Revenue ($millions)	Expenses ($millions)	Difference ($millions)
WWP	402.2	344.1	58.0
The Seminar Network, Inc.[a]	301.0	65.4	235.6
Veteran Tickets Foundation (Vet Tix)	171.6	168.2	3.3
DAV	147.4	149.2	(1.8)
PVA	127.0	109.3	17.8
VFW	98.1	95.7	2.4
U.S. VETS	76.8	76.7	0.1
Black Veterans for Social Justice, Inc.	63.1	62.2	0.9
Gary Sinise Foundation	60.4	59.2	1.2
The American Legion	58.1	68.6	(10.5)
Total	1,505.7	1,198.7	307.0

NOTE: Features information from organizations reporting in 2020 or later. Financials are from 2022 for all organizations except The Seminar Network, for which 2021 is the most recent information available and was converted into 2022 dollars. Numbers may not sum exactly due to rounding.

[a] The Seminar Network, formerly named Concerned Veterans for America, Inc., is a network of business leaders funded by Charles Koch and others that now operates as Stand Together; organizations can have up to four of these designations, and Stand Together may have selected W30 because a subgroup of Stand Together is Concerned Veterans for America.

TABLE 4.2

2022 Revenue and Expenses of Top Ten W30 Employment Organizations (by Revenue)

Organization	Revenue ($millions)	Expenses ($millions)	Difference ($millions)
U.S. VETS	76.8	76.7	0.1
The American Legion	58.1	68.6	(–10.5)
Black Veterans for Social Justice, Inc.	63.1	62.2	0.9
Swords to Plowshares Veterans Rights Organization	30.3	30.7	(0.3)
Veterans Village of San Diego	16.1	16.6	(0.5)
Veterans Multi-Service Center, Inc.	14.9	14.8	0.1
Bob Woodruff Family Foundation, Inc.	29.2	16.7	12.5
Warrior Canine Connection, Inc.	7.4	3.0	4.4
Purple Heart Homes, Inc.	6.0	6.1	(0.2)
Veterans Northeast Outreach Center, Inc.	4.5	5.0	(0.4)

SOURCE: Features information from organizations reporting in 2020 or later from Candid, undated. Financials are from 2022 for all organizations. Numbers may not sum exactly due to rounding.

TABLE 4.3
Revenue of Top Ten W30 Organizations in 2016 and 2022

Organization	2016 ($millions)	2022 ($millions)
WWP	276.5	402.2
DAV HQ	164.5	147.4
PVA HQ	127.2	127.0
VFW HQ	111.5	98.1
American Legion HQ	86.8	58.1
U.S. VETS	65.7	76.8
Operation Homefront[a]	55.0	63.0
Injured Marine Semper Fi Fund[a]	44.2	52.6
Support our Troops, Inc.[a]	41.0	30.5
Vet Tix	35.2	171.6

SOURCES: Features information from Moore et al., 2019; and Candid, undated.

NOTE: HQ = headquarters. Injured Marine Semper Fi Fund is now named Semper Fi & America's Fund.

[a] No longer in the top ten.

(in 2022 dollars; Giving USA, 2017) to $499 billion in 2022 (PNC Financial Services Group, 2023), an increase of just 8 percent. However, that overall growth trend obscures flat or declining revenue among some organizations (including established VSO headquarters) overshadowed by significant increases in others (including newer organizations, such as WWP and Vet Tix).

Employment-Focused Veteran-Serving Nonprofits

Chapter 2 documented our interviews with leaders of VSOs, funders, veteran leadership development programs, and employment-focused nonprofits. After these discussions, we developed a list of organizations mentioned in conversations as being active in helping veterans find employment or develop leadership skills. In Table 4.4, we show the revenue, expenses, NTEE code, and IRS tax exemption code of ten organizations for which it was possible to find information, as well as the expenses dedicated to employment-focused programming (when available) for organizations with broader missions.[2]

[2] We were unable to find financial information for some programs. For example, O2O is administered by Syracuse University's D'Aniello Institute for Veterans and Military Families, and the Focus Forward Fellowship is run by Purdue University's Military Family Research Institute; neither parent organization breaks out funding for these institutes or programs in their Form 990s or the audited financial reports posted online.

TABLE 4.4

2022 Revenue of Ten Employment or Leadership Development Veteran-Serving Nonprofits

Organization	Revenue ($millions)	Expenses ($millions)	NTEE Code[a]	IRS Code
U.S. Chamber of Commerce Foundation*	62.6	58.4	S41	501(c)(3)
HOH		11.1		
Hire Heroes USA	23.7	13.6	J22, P20	501(c)(3)
VetJobs*	5.4	4.2	S50	501(c)(3)
ACP Mentoring	7.3	4.9	J20	501(c)(3)
The OnwardOps Foundation	0.1	0.1		501(c)(3)
Black Veterans for Social Justice	63.1	62.2	W30	501(c)(3)
Employment		0.8		
The Mission Continues	18.6	11.3	S99	501(c)(3)
Travis Manion Foundation	11.1	8.5	P20, J21, O50	501(c)(4)
DAV HQ	147.4	149.2	W30	501(c)(3)
Employment		2.7		
WWP	402.1	344.1	W30, F30	501(c)(3)
Financial Wellness		37.0		

SOURCES: Features information from Candid, undated, for all except the U.S. Chamber of Commerce Foundation and the OnwardOps Foundation, which are from ProPublica, 2024b and ProPublica, 2024a, respectively. Black Veterans for Social Justice employment line item from Black Veterans for Social Justice, 2020. DAV line item for employment from DAV, 2022. WWP line item for financial wellness from WWP, 2023a. Financials are from 2022 for all organizations except those marked with an *, for which 2021 is the most recent information available; figures are presented in 2022 inflation-adjusted dollars.

[a] The definitions of these NTEE codes are presented in Appendix A.

Notably, none of these organizations is organized under 501(c)19. This suggests that they are not able to lobby and are not required to follow strict membership guidelines.

There are significant variations in the numbers of veterans served by programs, as well as the way those numbers are presented. As documented in Chapter 3, the HOH and Hire Heroes USA programs report more than 617,000 and 85,000 cumulative individuals hired, respectively; these organizations appear to be the most active among those that have a specific focus on employment. ACP reports that more than 30,000 veterans and spouses have completed mentorship; VetJobs reports 28,000 training classes completed in 2022 and just under 10.000 cumulative job placements. This list also includes organizations with broader missions; two have a leadership development element among their broader missions, The Mission Continues and Travis Manion Foundation. Notably, larger nonprofit organizations not only provide some employment-specific services to their own members but are also grantmaking organizations; for example, WWP lists several of these other organizations as grant recipients (WWP, 2023b).

Financials of Employment-Focused Veteran-Serving Nonprofits

We also reviewed the available annual financial reports of the veteran-serving nonprofits listed in Table 4.4 that have any employment focus. However, variations in how financial information is listed in the reviewed financial statements of nonprofits complicates efforts to provide accurate comparisons between them. For example, while most list grants and contributions separately, VetJobs combines them. Of those that do differentiate, reliance on grants varies substantially: Black Veterans for Social Justice and America's Corporate Partnership report 97 and 98 percent, respectively, of their revenues as coming from grants, compared with 70 percent at Hire Heroes USA; DAV reports no revenues from grants. DAV reports 52 percent of its revenue coming from donated services, contributions in kind, and donated media; most other organizations reported less than 2 percent of their total revenue in these categories.

There were significantly fewer differences in expenses between organizations: All spent more than 80 percent on program activities or services. DAV spent relatively more on fundraising, at 13 percent, while all other organizations spent 7 percent or less; all spent 9 percent or less on management, administration, and support services.

Another factor that significantly hinders the ability to accurately assess financial statements in the veteran-serving nonprofit space when it comes to organizations that support employment is that some organizations housed within other host institutions do not publicly release their information broken out separately (Institute for Veterans and Military Families, HOH) and likely absorb some overhead costs. For several others (DAV, Black Veterans for Social Justice), employment is only one line of effort among many, making it difficult to determine to what extent employment-focused services drive grants, contributions, and program service costs. Further complicating easy analysis of revenues and expenses within this sector, some large organizations (such as WWP and DAV) also give grants to other organizations.

Funding Compared with Need

If funding flows directed to organizations that support veteran employment were directly tied to demonstrable need, one might expect to see revenue to the sector rise with unemployment rates among veterans and fall when unemployment rates decline or, alternatively, for revenue to rise and fall with the number of transitioning service members.

However, that has not been the pattern since at least 2015, as shown in Figure 4.1. Rather, there has been a consistent upward trend in revenues in the veteran employment nonprofit sector. At the same time, veteran unemployment generally declined, with the notable exception of a significant unemployment spike during the COVID-19 pandemic. This has remained true even as the number of service members transitioning out of the military annually has also decreased during that time. Veteran unemployment has remained below nonveteran

FIGURE 4.1
Veteran Unemployment and Number of Active-Duty Separations Annually Versus Revenue to the Sector (2022 Inflation-Adjusted Dollars)

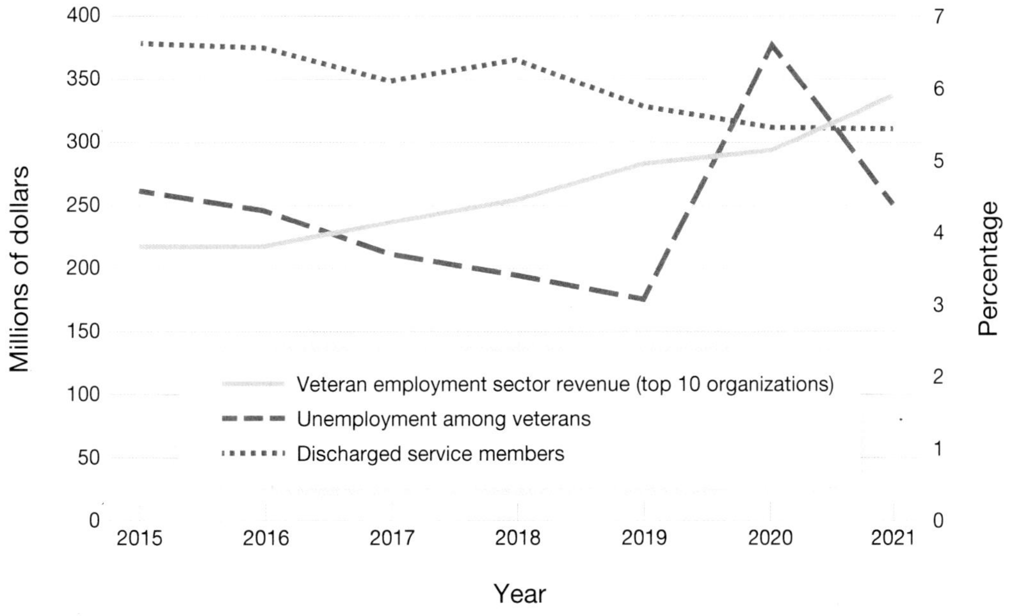

SOURCES: Features information from Candid, undated, for veteran employment sector revenue; U.S. Bureau of Labor Statistics, 2023, for unemployment rates; and DoD annual demographics reports, for number of discharged service members, from Military OneSource, undated.

unemployment throughout this time. Notably, the total unemployment rate cannot capture higher rates of unemployment within subpopulations of veterans or rates of underemployment, two other issues that some of these nonprofits seek to address and for which they may actively solicit funding. Much more goes into shaping revenue levels among these organizations, and this is not meant as a comprehensive analysis; rather, the figure simply illustrates that revenues in the sector that supports veteran employment are shaped by myriad complex factors, and not simply current unemployment levels. Public perceptions shaped by coverage of high unemployment rates in the past may also continue to shape behavior.

Conclusion

The number of transitioning service members and veteran unemployment have both declined, as shown in Figure 4.1. It follows that the employment-focused sector of the veteran-serving nonprofit space could have declined as well. In Table 4.5, we show change over the six-year period from 2016 to 2022 for the groupings of organizations discussed above: the ten largest W30 organizations by revenue now and in the 2019 CNAS report, the ten largest W30 organizations with an explicit employment focus listed, the Big 6 VSO Headquarters, and

TABLE 4.5
Revenue and Revenue Change in Employment Organizations and Other Subgroups (Using 2022 Inflation-Adjusted Dollars)

	Top 10 Veteran Employment W30 Orgs	Top 10 Veteran-Sector W30 Orgs	Top 10 2019 CNAS Report W30 Orgs	"Big Six" HQs	Top 10 High-Activity Veteran Employment Orgs	Charitable Sector Overall
2022 revenue ($millions)	307	1,506	1,227	445	742	499,330
Change (2016–2022, $millions)	189	513	143	(53)	123	36,108
Change (2016–2022, %)	28.99	34.06	11.65	−11.91	16.58	7.79
Change per year (%)	4.83	5.68	1.94	−1.99	2.76	1.56

NOTE: HQs = headquarters; orgs = organizations.

ten high-activity veteran employment–focused nonprofits overall for which revenue can be found (those shown in Table 4.2), along with the charitable sector overall.

Overall, the trends over this six-year period indicate that revenue for all examined subsets of the veteran-serving nonprofit sector except for the Big Six VSOs has been increasing (the decline in revenue for the Big Six VSOs may be in part because they are member-based organizations, and the size of the veteran population has been declining). This growth has been faster than revenue for the broader nonprofit sector and sometimes substantially so. These trends do not seem to fully support concerns raised during interviews about future sustainability for the sector.

However, specific organizations are not assured survival. While giving overall has continued to increase, individual organizations have seen substantial—in some cases, dramatic—declines in revenue. This is particularly true for the traditional VSOs, which can lobby for legislation that could benefit veterans, including that which would provide government grants for programs that support veterans. Smaller organizations may be better served by consolidating to reduce duplication of effort and/or overhead. Chapter-based organizations may need to carefully consider projected demographics of the veteran population nationwide and collaborate to plan for a right-sized future. Organizations that are heavily reliant on corporate or foundation grants may benefit from diversifying their revenue streams. Additionally, recent trends do not assure future prospects: Giving priorities may shift. In the next chapter, we present the findings of a survey about individual charitable giving to support veterans, which may represent an underexploited avenue to balance sources of revenue.

CHAPTER 5

Public Sentiment on Charitable Giving to Support Veterans

R. Gordon Rinderknecht and Meredith Kleykamp

In this chapter, we again turn to recent concerns held by some in the veteran-serving nonprofit sector about the future of philanthropic funding for their organizations. The previous chapter examined this uncertainty through quantitative queries of these organizations' overall revenues. Here, we look through the lens of individual giving, which is the source of 64 percent of all philanthropic donations in the broader charitable sector (Gaumer, 2023). We did so by leveraging the RAND American Life Panel (ALP), a nationally representative, probability-based panel of U.S. adults that has been used to conduct more than 450 surveys covering diverse topics of concern to Americans. We focused on the future prospects of individual donations, which is Research Question 4:

Research Question 4

Donation prospects. What are the prospects for future charitable giving to veterans' causes?

In fall 2023, we asked participants about the future viability of charities supporting veteran causes relative to other causes, including emerging public concerns. Further, we added measures capturing attitudes relevant to charitable giving and veterans' issues to identify the priorities of those who do and do not donate to veteran-serving organizations. We then compared the responses of those who financially support veterans' issues. This was done to discern those who reported a large or small proportion of their total charitable giving to veterans' issues because a greater percentage of giving may indicate a stronger connection to veterans. This could signal different attitudes regarding veteran support.

The RAND American Life Panel: Data and Methodology

This chapter presents findings from Wave #615 of the ALP, conducted in fall 2023. This survey was designed by RAND researchers to assess respondents' general charitable giving behaviors, as well as those related more specifically to veterans' issues. The ALP includes more than 6,000 members aged 18 and older. Respondents are regularly interviewed over the internet, allowing us to link our primary analysis of ALP Wave #615 with relevant survey measures collected in previous waves. Specifically, our supplemental analyses are supported by measures merged from ALP waves measuring veteran stereotypes (#591), military affiliation (#574), and political affiliation (#566 and #546) (Kleykamp, Schwam, and Wenig, 2023; Helmus, Brown, and Ramchand, 2023)

The ALP is representative of the civilian, residential population aged 18 and older. The ALP, as is typical with representative surveys, does not match its reference population. The ALP therefore provides weights that increase or decrease the influence of any single response, with greater (lesser) emphasis placed on responses from underrepresented (overrepresented) groups—culminating in an overall sample that closely matches its benchmark, the Current Population Survey Annual Social and Economic Supplement, in terms of gender, age, ethnicity, education, household income, and number of household members. (For more information on how these weights are constructed, see Pollard and Baird, 2017.) All analyses use these provided weights.

In our primary survey (ALP #615), respondents reported which categories of charitable giving they donated to in the previous 12 months (question 1) and the amount they donate to charities annually (question 2). Our questions then focused specifically on charitable giving to veterans' issues. We asked respondents what percentage of their charitable giving goes to veterans' issues (question 3), and their attitudes regarding how veterans' issues should be funded, with options ranging from "exclusively federal funding" to "exclusively private charitable giving" (question 4). Next, respondents reported the kinds of veterans' issues that should receive the most charitable giving (question 5), the kinds of veterans and families who should receive the most charitable giving (question 6), and how respondents anticipated their charitable giving to veterans' issues would change in the coming years (question 7). Lastly, respondents reported the most important factors affecting their decisions to financially support a charitable organization (question 8). Of the 3,704 people who were invited to take the survey, 2,000 people took the survey, for a 54-percent completion rate. Of these 2,000 respondents, 108 were removed because of incomplete data or incorrect reporting, leaving us with an analytic sample size of 1,892 respondents.

We were primarily interested in three kinds of respondents: those who donate a high percentage of their overall giving to veterans' issues ("Donates to Vet Issues [large %]"), those who donate a low percentage of their overall giving to veterans' issues ("Donates to Vet Issues [small %]"), and those who donate nothing to veterans' issues ("Does Not Donate to Vet Issues"). We defined 25 percent or greater as *large* (and a *low* percentage as under 25 percent) because this cutoff divided those who donate to veterans' issues into two similarly sized groups. We break down our presentation of questions 4 through 8 by our three giving categories. We further provide a supplemental analysis (see Appendix G) of question 8 separating those who do not give to veterans' issues into two categories: those who donate a large amount of money (greater than $1,000 over the past 12 months) to other charitable causes, and those who donate less or were unsure how much they donated. We test for statistically significant differences between these groups via bivariate regression analyses (discussed in the footnote of each figure).

Our supplemental analyses (see Appendix G) also indicate how our three giving categories differ in terms of veteran stereotypes, military affiliation, and political affiliation. To provide these comparisons, we merged earlier ALP waves into our analytic sample. Political affiliation is merged from ALP #566 and #546—if a respondent was in both #566 and #546, we used the most recent response from #566. Military affiliation was merged from ALP #574, and perceptions of veteran stereotypes was merged from ALP #591. We examine the cumulative linked sample of 826 respondents in the supplementary section.

Charitable Giving Behaviors

The individual support provided to veteran-serving nonprofit organizations is comparable to that given to organizations supporting many other causes. Figure 5.1 shows that 14 percent of respondents gave to a veteran-serving charity in the previous 12 months. This is on par with the percentage who gave to charities focused on health and disease and civil rights, and greater than the percentage who donated to climate and environmental issues. Yet, giving to veteran-serving charities is far behind giving to human services, religious organizations, other kinds of charities (such as arts, disaster relief, education, and international aid), and charities focused on animals (such as wildlife conservation and animal shelters). We explore the different priorities of respondents who give a large percentage of their total giving to veterans' issues, those who give a small percentage of their total giving to veterans' issues, and those who give nothing to veterans' issues in the next section. (See Figure G.1 in Appendix G for a breakdown of the percentage of total giving that goes to veterans' issues among those who give anything to support veterans' issues.)

Attitudes Regarding Charitable Giving to Veterans

Most survey respondents feel the federal government should take the lead in support for veterans' issues. Figure 5.2 indicates that most respondents prefer that veterans' issues be funded primarily by the federal government, supplemented by private charitable giving.[1]

[1] This aligns with the current status quo: Revenue to W30-coded nonprofits in 2022 was $4.28 billion, according to our analysis, while, in the same year, the VA budget was $270 billion.

FIGURE 5.1
Proportion of Respondents Who Donate to Each Cause

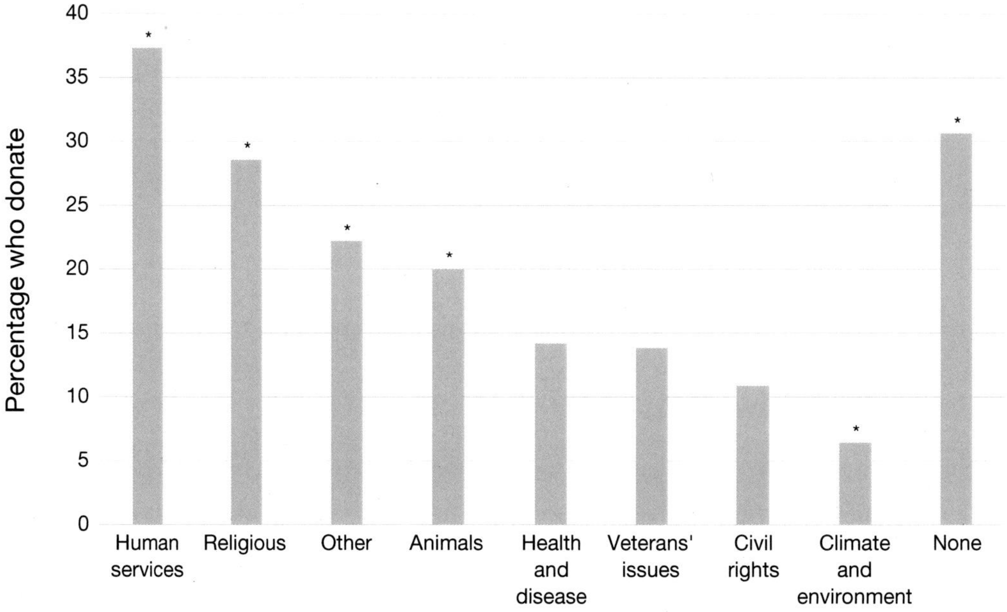

SOURCE: Features data from ALP #615 (2023). N = 1,892.
NOTE: All estimates are weighted. * indicates the charitable cause differs significantly from giving to veterans' issues.

Almost no respondents prefer veterans' issues be supported mostly or entirely by private charitable giving. These attitudes do not vary significantly between giving categories.

Veteran employment issues come in fourth among veteran-related issues that donors support most. Figure 5.3 shows that attitudes also vary little between giving categories when respondents report which veterans' issues should receive the most charitable giving. The dominant issues among all groups are mental health, housing, and physical health. Employment then came in fourth overall, with 25 percent of respondents who donate a large percentage of their charitable giving to veterans' issues selecting employment as a top issue, followed by 22 percent among those who donate nothing to veterans' issues, and 13 percent among those who donate a small percentage of their charitable giving to veterans' issues. The only significant group difference relates to those who donate a small proportion of their total giving to veterans' issues, in that they place greater importance on recreational activities relative to the other giving categories. Figure 5.4 shows a similarly high level of agreement on who should receive the most charitable giving, with responses dominated by injured veterans and the families of those who died in service. Respondents who donate to veterans' issues reported significantly greater focus on injured veterans than did those who do not donate to veterans' issues, while those who do not donate to veterans' issues generally placed more importance on post-9/11 veterans and veterans who separated from the military with an Other Than

FIGURE 5.2

Preferred Sources of Funding for Veterans' Issues

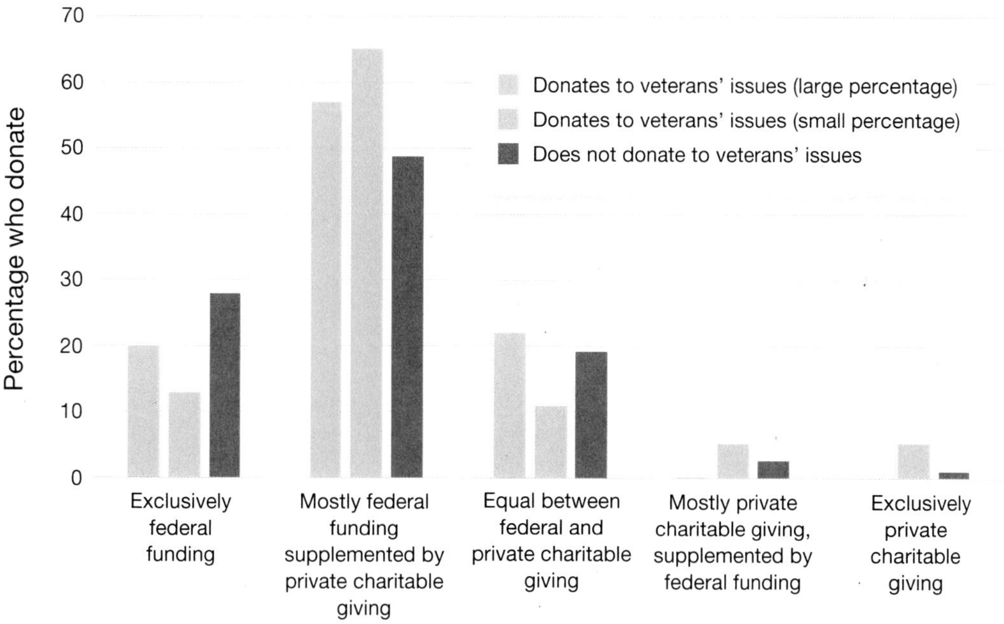

SOURCE: Features data from ALP #615 (2023). $N = 1{,}892$.

NOTE: All estimates are weighted. Differences between giving categories were tested with a bivariate ordinary least squares regression with respondents' preferred source of funding as the dependent variable and giving category as the independent variable. There are no statistically significant differences in preferred sources of funding for veterans' issues between giving categories.

Honorable discharge classification (often known as having "bad papers"). Note, however, that a relatively small percentage of respondents across all groups selected these two options.

Survey participants feel they will continue to give to veteran-serving organizations in the future. Figure 5.5 shows that virtually no respondents expect to give less to veterans' issues in the future. Most commonly, respondents across all giving categories expect to continue giving at their current rates, and those who give a small percentage of their total giving to veterans' issues plan to give significantly more than those who currently give nothing to veterans' issues.

Factors Affecting Charitable Giving Decisions

People mainly donate to charitable causes because they are interested in the cause and feel connected to the organizations. Figure 5.6 shows the most-important factors affecting respondents' decisions to give to a charitable organization. The dominant reasons given here are interest in the cause or issue and connection to the organization.

FIGURE 5.3
Attitudes Regarding Which Veterans' Issues Should Receive the Most Charitable Giving

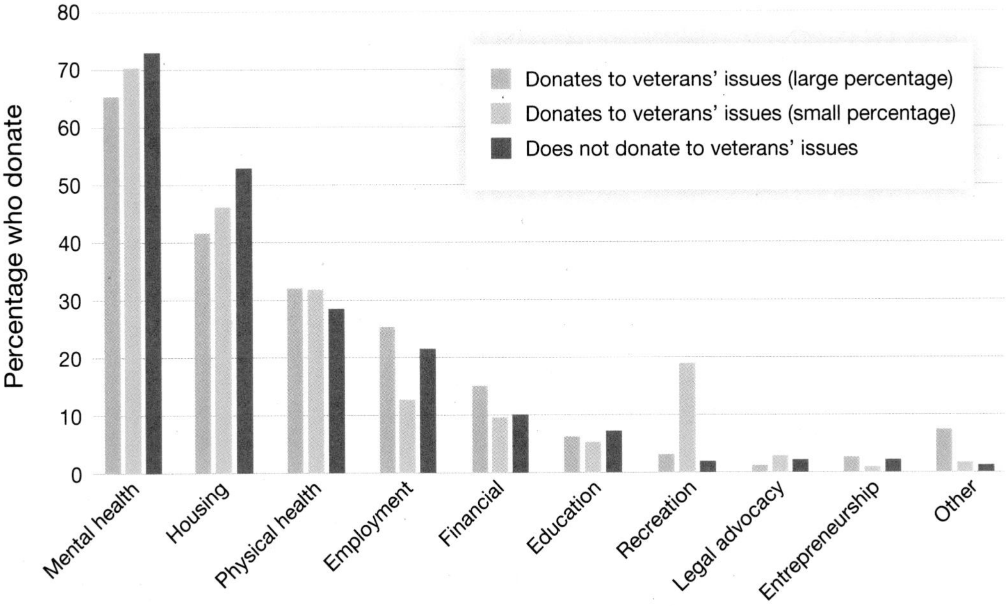

SOURCE: Features data from ALP #615 (2023). N = 1,892.

NOTE: All estimates are weighted. Respondents reported their top two choices. Differences between giving categories were tested with multiple bivariate logistic regressions, with respondents' selection of each issue as the dependent variable and giving category as the independent variable. The only significant group difference relates to recreation, in which those who donate a small proportion of their total giving to veterans' issues place greater importance on recreational activities relative to the other giving categories.

There are nuances in the reasons people give or do not give to a cause. There are some notable differences between giving categories in the importance of these factors. Respondents who do not donate to veterans' issues reported placing significantly more importance on recommendations and significantly less importance on direct solicitations from charitable organizations relative to both veteran-supporting groups. Further, respondents who direct a large percentage of their giving to veterans' issues reported placing significantly more importance on their interest in the cause relative to those who give nothing to veterans' issues. We further assess the motivations of those who do not give to veterans' issues by separating those who give $1,000 or more to non-veteran-supporting charities from others who do not give to veteran-supporting charities (see Figures G.2 and G.3 in Appendix G).

Conclusion

Among our survey respondents, individual giving to veterans' issues is on par with or exceeds recent areas of public concern. These respondents generally recognize the importance of pri-

FIGURE 5.4
Attitudes Regarding Which Kinds of Veterans Should Receive the Most Charitable Giving

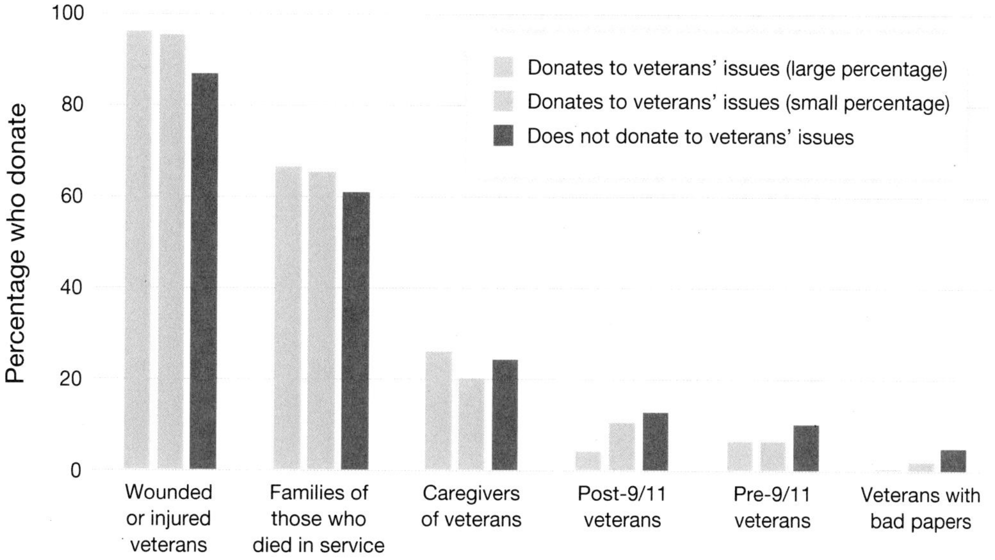

SOURCE: Features data from ALP #615 (2023). *N* = 1,892.
NOTE: All estimates are weighted. Respondents reported their top two choices. Differences between giving categories were tested with multiple bivariate logistic regressions with respondents' selection of each kind of veteran as the dependent variable and giving category as the independent variable. Both veteran-supporting groups reported significantly greater focus on wounded veterans than did those who do not donate to veterans' issues, while those who do not donate to veterans' issues placed more importance on post-9/11 veterans and veterans with bad papers relative to respondents who give a large percentage of their giving to veterans' issues.

vate charitable giving to support veterans' issues, and we see no evidence that these respondents expect to decrease their charitable giving in the near term. In fact, a large proportion of the sample expect to give more in the future.

Our supplementary analysis highlights, however, that charitable giving to veterans' issues is significantly related to the donor's connection to the military, either directly or through other family members. Should this connection decline over the long term, interest in charitable giving to veterans' issues may also decline. This decline in charitable giving may be avoided by increased donations from those who already give to veterans' issues, since such givers tend to direct only a small proportion of their total charitable giving, at the time of writing, to support veterans. A greater focus on veterans' issues and the kinds of veterans perceived as most in need may also be beneficial for eliciting further charitable giving.

Another avenue to diversify revenue streams and enhance overall sustainability within the sector could be enhanced collaboration with the public sector, to which we turn in the next chapter.

FIGURE 5.5
Respondents' Anticipated Future Giving to Veterans' Issues

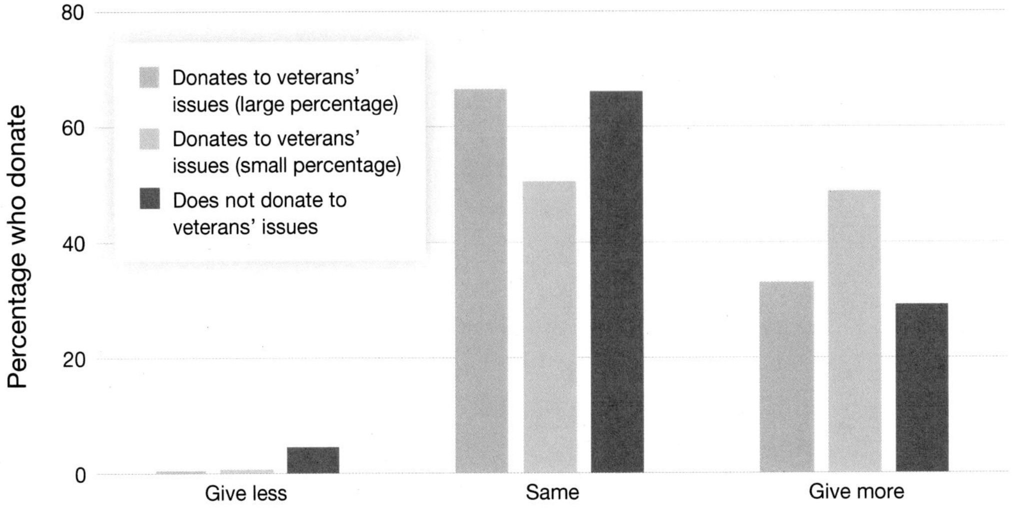

SOURCE: Features data from ALP #615 (2023). N = 1,892.

NOTE: All estimates are weighted. Differences between giving categories were tested with a bivariate ordered logistic regression with respondents' decision to give less, the same, or more in the future as the dependent variable and giving category as the independent variable. Those who direct a small percentage of their total giving to veterans' issues plan to give significantly more than those who currently give nothing to veterans' issues. Those who direct a large percentage of their total giving to veterans' issues do not differ significantly from other giving categories.

FIGURE 5.6

Most Important Factors Affecting Respondents' Charitable Giving Decisions

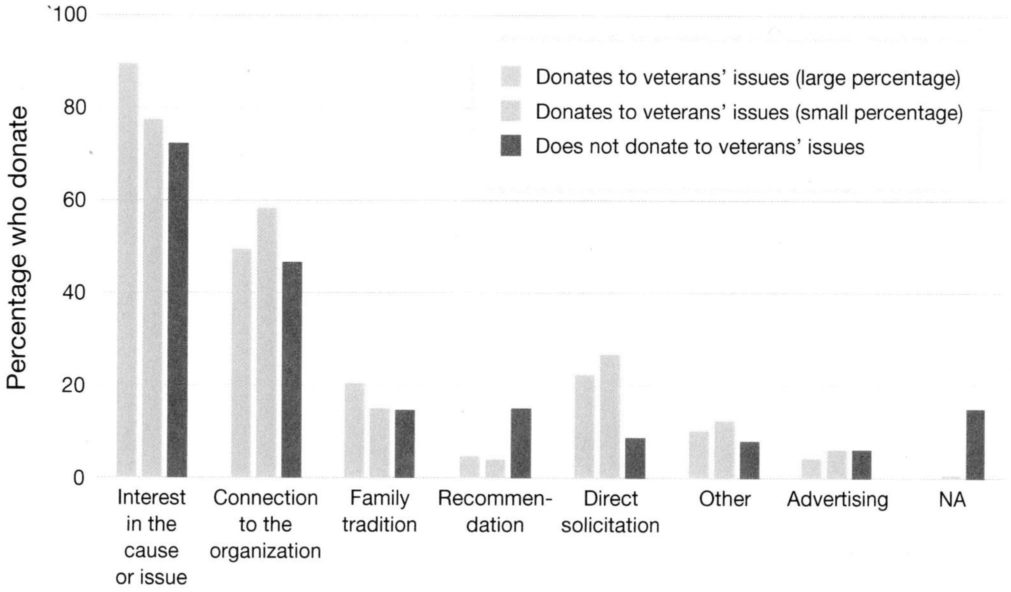

SOURCE: Features data from ALP #615 (2023). *N* = 1,892.

NOTE: All estimates are weighted. Respondents reported their top two choices. Differences between giving categories were tested with multiple bivariate logistic regressions with respondents' selection of each factor as the dependent variable and giving category as the independent variable. Respondents who do not donate to veterans' issues reported placing significantly more importance on recommendations and significantly less importance on direct solicitations from charitable organizations relative to both veteran-supporting groups. Respondents who direct a large percentage of their giving to veterans' issues reported placing significantly more importance on their interest in the cause relative to those who give nothing to veterans' issues. Relative to other giving categories, respondents who give nothing to veterans' issues were more likely to select *NA*, indicating that they give nothing to charity.

CHAPTER 6

The Role of Public-Private Partnerships to Support Veteran Employment

Brandon F. De Bruhl

Governments, community organizations, and private institutions frequently collaborate for various reasons. These collaborations leverage diverse resources, expertise, and local community relationships (Abdel-Samad et al., 2021; Beall et al., 2019). VA, for example, operates within a complex ecosystem of nonprofit and private-sector service providers to facilitate veteran health care, employment, and transition to civilian life and has done so since the early 20th century (see Appendix H for a history of this ecosystem). In 2023, VA provided $2.36 billion in funding to nonprofits via grants and contracts (VA, National Center for Healthcare Advancement and Partnerships, 2024). VA has developed grants to support services for veterans, including burial services and adaptive sports programs, legal services, and community support for those at risk of homelessness. For instance, VA has awarded grants to organizations providing transitional housing and other services to eligible veterans under the Grant and Per Diem program since 1994. Under the Staff Sergeant Parker Gordon Fox Suicide Prevention Grant Program (VA, 2023), Congress authorized VA to issue $174 million in grants of up to $750,000 to community-based organizations providing or coordinating suicide prevention services to at-risk veterans and their families, particularly in rural communities, on tribal lands, or in other areas with limited access to medical services.

Public-private partnerships (P3) are crucial in helping VA and other federal agencies fulfill their missions to support veteran employment. This chapter explores these partnerships, first identifying and evaluating different types of P3 models and then providing recommen-

> **Research Question 5**
>
> **Federal agency collaboration.** How do veteran-serving nonprofits collaborate with government agencies, and what are the challenges with public-private partnerships?

dations for how the federal government can strengthen its relationships with nonprofit programs working to support veteran employment.

Evaluating the Modern Public-Private Partnership Typologies

To better understand the P3 ecosystem, we analyzed the research literature on P3s. However, unlike a traditional literature review, we explored what the literature had to say about the types of organizations within the P3 ecosystem and what barriers they may face in interacting with the government.

We used a *text-as-data* approach for our analysis, which involves treating text data from the literature as counts or frequencies to evaluate observable trends or patterns. This method has gained popularity because of the vast amount of text data that are now digitally accessible, necessitating new techniques for accessing and analyzing such data. By transforming text into quantitative data, researchers can aggregate and identify features within a body of literature, uncovering insights that might be missed through traditional qualitative analysis.

The analysis involved several steps. First, we used an Application Program Interface (API) to access relevant articles, selecting those that matched our inclusion and exclusion criteria.[1] We used three different literature databases: Web of Science API, Elsevier Research API, and Semantic Scholar API. This initial search yielded 3,451 articles, which were narrowed down to 432 based on their relevance to the relationship between government and nongovernmental organizations, including private entities, nonprofits, and community service organizations. Next, we processed the text data to extract counts and frequencies of key terms and concepts. This quantitative analysis allowed us to identify recurring themes and challenge areas within the literature. For instance, we could observe how often certain challenges, such as administrative burdens or transaction costs, were mentioned and how these challenges were framed in different contexts.

Types of Public-Private Partnerships

Using the text-as-data approach, we analyzed the literature on P3s and identified three main P3 typologies: asset, contract, and service (Table 6.1). *Asset* P3s focus on serving as a guardian for a specific asset or a collection of similar assets, e.g., a consortium of government, private companies, and public conservatories for a newly built bridge. In *contract* P3s, the government seeks to achieve a predetermined target outcome. In *service* P3s, the govern-

[1] Inclusion criteria focused on studies examining the dynamics and relationships between domestic (city, state, federal) government entities and P3 institutions, particularly in multiperiod interactions. Relevant sectors were infrastructure, health care, education, and veteran services. We included qualitative, quantitative, and mixed-method studies, case studies, and comparative analyses. We excluded studies focusing on intra-organizational dynamics, international P3, and interactions involving nongovernmental organizations if they also included P3 institutions. Additionally, studies addressing private-sector interactions without P3s were excluded.

TABLE 6.1
Typology of P3 Organizations

Typology Name	Description	Example
Asset P3	Focuses on managing and maintaining specific assets or a collection of assets	A consortium of government, private companies, and public conservatories managing a newly built bridge
Contract P3	Involves predefined outputs and specific deliverables as per a contractual agreement	An agreement that requires participating organizations to place 50 new job openings within an annual performance period
Service P3	Centers on provision of ongoing activities and services without predefined outputs	Education and vocational training programs that provide skill development and job placement

ment establishes a persistent, ongoing relationship with a longer-term target outcome. We found that contract- and service-types are the most prevalent forms of P3s related to veteran employment.[2] These typologies give us a starting point for analyzing some core challenges that might appear.

Public-Private Partnership Challenges

Our literature search revealed multiple types of challenges with P3 arrangements, which we normatively analyzed to identify recurring themes in the P3 literature. Many of these challenges stem from administrative and organizational issues arising from interactions between the government and P3 organizations. The following section briefly describes the themes found in the computational literature review.

Asymmetric Information and Principal-Agent Problems

Asymmetric information is a significant challenge in P3s. It occurs when one party, typically the private entity, has more information about project costs, risks, or performance than the government (Gallouj, 1997; Lambert, Leuz, and Verrecchia, 2012). This imbalance can lead to suboptimal decisionmaking, because the government may not have all the necessary information to make informed choices. Additionally, asymmetric information can increase project risks and costs, since the government might underestimate potential issues or overestimate the capabilities of the private partner (Xiong, Zhao, and Wang, 2018). Addressing

[2] To assess this, we counted the number of articles' keywords that used *P3* under our framework. Of the 432 articles in our dataset, we found a cross-section of articles focused on health care P3s, of which 116 (27 percent) described a service-type, and 71 (17 percent) described a contract-type. We also found that among a cross-section of articles on employment-focused P3s, 97 (22 percent) described a service-type and 47 (11 percent) described a contract-type. There was a small percentage of articles that dealt with asset typologies—about 53 (12 percent), which was lower than anticipated. However, a quick examination showed that the asset literature was predominantly associated with private peer-to-peer firms and governments, which likely were eliminated by the exclusion criteria.

information asymmetry involves enhancing transparency, improving communication channels, and ensuring that both parties have access to accurate and comprehensive data.

An important form of information asymmetry is the principal-agent problem (Tipu and Yousaf, 2022; Moore and Vining, 2023). In this framing, the principal (often the government) seeks a benefit from an agent (e.g., a nonprofit organization); the government has a limited capability to monitor the agent and must trust that the agent will do what is asked (Silaghi and Sarkar, 2021). The solution is to align the interests of the principal and the agent—for example, by providing an incentive, such as compensation, to the agent to complete the requested action (Rybnicek, Plakolm, and Baumgartner, 2020). There may be incentive structures other than compensation that could work to address this challenge. For example, in some cases, the principal could rely on a shared sense of mission to ensure the intended activity is completed (Cao, Li, and Su, 2024).

Without aligning interests—for example, by underproviding compensation in terms of money, resources, and labor—the principal causes the agent to engage in satisficing behavior, by which it seeks satisfactory rather than optimal results (Altman, 2008). This often leads to the agent shirking on deliverables and struggling to meet the agreement's requirements (Miller and Whitford, 2007). Persistent inadequate compensation devalues the agent's work because its actual costs are not fully covered. Principals, especially in government programs, may undervalue the agent's efforts because of budget constraints and the need to make trade-offs between programs (Grossman and Hart, 1992; Ross, 1973). This results in minimized payments for services provided by the agent and can effectively create unfunded mandates, increased administrative burdens, and information gaps, consuming resources that could support the P3 ecosystem.

Transaction Costs and Administrative Burden

A second theme in our literature analysis was that transaction costs can be a critical challenge for P3 arrangements. Transaction costs refer to the expenses incurred during the negotiation, monitoring, and enforcement of contracts between public and private entities (Williamson and Masten, 1999). These costs can significantly affect the overall efficiency and effectiveness of the partnership. High transaction costs can arise from prolonged contract negotiations, extensive monitoring and compliance requirements, and legal disputes (Iossa and Martimort, 2015). Transaction costs are often transferred to agents, which increases the actual costs to the agent of providing the service. In response, agents may resist new administrative demands, such as for increased reporting about performing, which in turn reduces the principal's information about whether the partnership is meeting its objectives.

To minimize transaction costs, it is essential for the government to streamline contract processes, establish clear and efficient monitoring systems, and foster a cooperative relationship between the public and private partners (Vining, Boardman, and Poschmann, 2005). Reducing transaction costs can enhance the operational efficiency of P3 projects, allowing more resources to be allocated toward achieving the partnership's goals.

Administrative burden is a special type of transaction cost associated with additional workload and bureaucratic processes required to manage, monitor, and regulate partnerships. These burdens can include extensive paperwork, complex reporting requirements, and the need for constant oversight, all of which can strain the resources of both public and private entities (Herd and Moynihan, 2019). High administrative burdens can reduce the efficiency of P3 projects, diverting time and resources away from core activities and potentially leading to delays and increased costs. Addressing administrative burdens is essential to improve the overall efficiency and success of P3, ensuring that both parties can focus on delivering effective and timely outcomes.

Administrative Design and Financial Delivery

The third theme we found in the P3 literature centers on organizational challenges, including the concepts of administrative design and financial delivery. When the government needs to leverage P3 relationships, it needs to understand the organizational and funding pressures that will be placed on the delivery partners by the relationship (Rachwalski and Ross, 2010).

Administrative design refers to how the principal and agent are organizationally structured. In P3 arrangements to provide social services, such as veteran employment, the P3 partners are often nonprofit organizations. To meet the reporting and regulatory requirements of the government, many nonprofit organizations would need to change certain aspects of their organizational structure, such as having certain policies and procedures in place or changing the business model. When a nongovernment partner is not organized to effectively work within the government process and meet the administrative constraints, the resulting P3 relationship is far less likely to succeed (Rybnicek, Plakolm, and Baumgartner, 2020). Administrative design matters for both the government and the nonprofit partner, because each must be willing to take on some risk of delivering the service to improve outcomes (Murphy, 2008; Liang and Ashuri, 2022). Well-functioning P3 arrangements manifest as organizational change when the government becomes more flexible in its administrative requirements and P3 partners become more specialized in collaborating with the government's administrative needs (Galvin, Tywoniak, and Sutherland, 2021).

Financial delivery refers to the fact that partner organizations must trust the government to be a responsible fiscal partner. Nonprofit P3 partners offer a service that has community demand but either high fixed cost or high-variance variable costs (Kingma, 1997; Boardman and Vining, 2010; Ilhan, 2013). For financial stability, low-margin nonprofits need to find a stable fiscal partner (Talavera and Sanchis, 2020). The government P3 partnership can serve as a fiscal anchor institution to these organizations, enabling the reduction of high capital costs by covering startup costs or providing stable, moderate long-run support, which reduces fiscal variance (Smith and Lipsky, 2009; Weisbrod, 2009; Guo and Acar, 2005).

Challenges by Type of Public-Private Partnership

Our evaluation also examined the frequency of each challenge area associated with each P3 typology. The basic approach involved using a word search to categorize each article into a typology category and determine the frequency of words related to each problem area. This process used foundational natural language processing techniques to tokenize the words based on a provided dictionary (Gentzkow, Kelly, and Taddy, 2019; Grimmer, Roberts, and Stewart, 2022). Each tokenized word was assigned a score ranging from 0 to 1. Articles with higher frequencies of keywords related to the identified challenges received higher scores, while those with fewer relevant keywords received lower scores. These scores were then converted into percentages and reported in Figure 6.1.

We note that a limitation of this type of analysis is that it includes only the findings reported in the research literature and may not be representative of all P3 arrangements. For example, researchers could happen to publish more studies about one type of challenge, which could overweight that topic in the overall analysis. Therefore, these scores are descriptive evaluations of our study corpus and do not indicate a causal relationship. Instead, they serve to highlight trends in the identified challenge areas relative to the typologies.

As noted earlier, our analysis suggests that service and contract types largely dominate the veteran employment P3 ecosystem. We can see that information asymmetry, administrative burden, transaction costs, and administrative design all show up in these two types. In implementing P3s, the federal government should be cognizant that it could be discounting the actual value that P3 partners bring to the table either by undercompensating or imposing additional administrative burdens. In the next section, we consider how to analyze several recent pilot programs under this framework.

FIGURE 6.1
Challenges by P3 Type

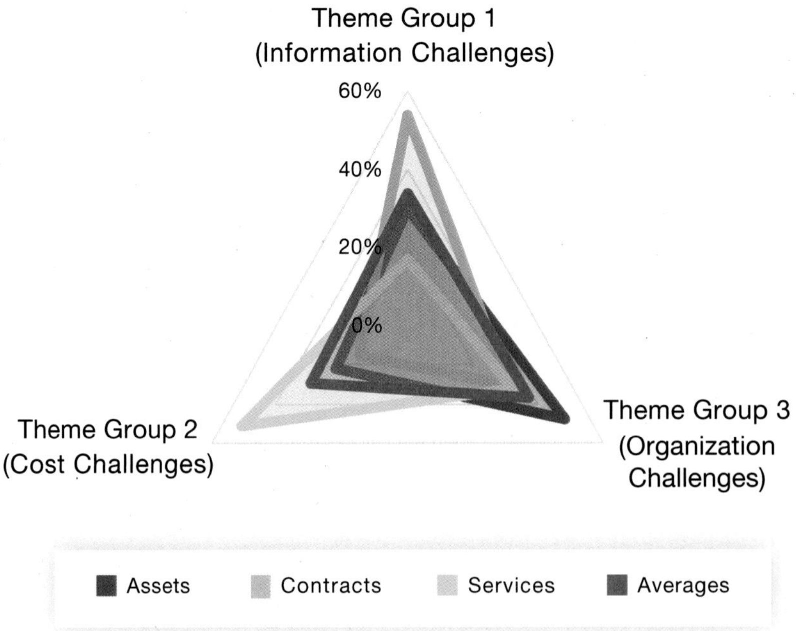

Considerations for Current and Future Public-Private Partnerships to Support Veteran Employment

As seen in the model and typologies, there is tension between federal agencies, such as VA and DoL, and the veteran nonprofit organization community. P3s are currently underutilized in the veteran transition and employment sector. Administrative burdens can cause programs to be underutilized, as the extensive paperwork, complex reporting requirements, and constant oversight demands can deter organizations from fully participating. These burdens can strain the resources of both public and private entities, diverting time and effort from core activities and reducing the overall effectiveness of the programs. The government is likely underestimating the anticipated administrative burden associated with grant programs within the P3 ecosystem, leading to a mismatch between the program's design and the capacity of organizations to comply with administrative requirements.

Our analytical framework can provide insight into some of challenges inherent in current federal P3 ecosystem partnerships, including two example P3s: the Employment Navigator and Partnership Program (ENPP) and the Veteran and Spouse Transitional Assistance Grant Program.

DoL's Employment Navigator and Partnership Program

Employment placement activities fall into the contract-type category. The ENPP is a pilot program that provides a clearinghouse of job-related information to support transition. The ENPP's annual appropriation includes provisions for apprenticeship placements and coordinating handovers from the American Job Centers, with funding of around $31 million in 2022 (DoL, Veterans' Employment and Training Service, undated). One mechanism this program uses is connecting the veteran job seeker with local P3 organizations that both provide individualized information and help connect the candidate to the job market. The ENPP requires P3 organizations to complete an application and meet program standards for placement services. Essentially, DoL-ENPP forms a contract with the P3 organization by which ENPP provides clients who meet the program's workforce and education standards, and the P3 organizations work as agents providing pathways to employment.

A tension point within the program is that, while the ENPP receives budget support for its main education programs, the P3 organizations supporting placement and information are not directly funded by this program. As noted in our discussion of contract-type P3s, financial burden and information asymmetry are key concerns. The ENPP relies on the P3 organizations to have sufficient resources to place all the candidates, putting the resource burden on the P3 organizations to seek outside funding or lower the quality of placements. This dynamic can result in the agency meeting program objectives at the cost of the P3 organizations, which may eventually leave the contract.

VA's Proposed Veteran and Spouse Transitional Assistance Grant Program

In May 2024, the VA announced its plans to establish the Veteran and Spouse Transitional Assistance Grant Program, which supports the transition of military personnel and their spouses to the civilian workforce ("Veteran and Spouse Transitional Assistance Grant Program," undated). These grants are intended to enable eligible P3 organizations to fund transition services (i.e., résumé assistance, interview training, and job placement services); intensive client case support (i.e., career counseling, skill development, and mentorship programs); and outreach engagement, such as activity, placement promotion, and business collaborations. Each P3 organization will apply through a Notice of Funding Opportunity (NOFO), whereby each grant application will outline the use of these funds to facilitate one or more desired transition support services (VA, 2024). The selection process is scored based on the NOFO, and each applicant is ranked according to that score. Grant selection criteria are oriented to benefit programs that provide multiple services, locations with large veteran populations, states with high rates of veteran unemployment assistance programs, and states that were adversely affected or are still affected by COVID-19.

This program falls under our contract typology, and its design highlights some of the concerns found in our literature analysis. As noted above, the contract type is susceptible to principal-agent dynamics and asymmetry of information. There are several mechanisms within the rulemaking that suggest potential challenges. First, the dominant role of the NOFO is to prescribe maximum funds per grant; the sequencing of money over an unspecified period means that the monitoring criteria are susceptible to principal-agent issues. This creates uncertainty within the agents (grantees) as to whether they will be reauthorized for the next period. This opens the door for grantees to limit their commitment to the program, focusing less on meeting evaluation metrics and more on securing future funding opportunities.

Secondly, there is informational asymmetry around which organization can and should access these program funds. Potential grantees theoretically include all states, nonprofits, and faith-based institutions. However, the selection preference for programs seems to be larger organizations that have the capabilities and established resources to deliver on multiple programs. The geographic requirements also seem to give preference to states that are more likely to have pre-established traditional transition benefit programs. While the NOFO is an important tool for managing the grant program, there is a great deal of informational uncertainty regarding who should be qualified and selected for the program.

Conclusions

The P3 typologies provide a framework for identifying potential challenges to current and new federal initiatives that support veteran transition and employment. Several qualitative factors stand out in our literature analysis, including principal-agent dynamics, informational asymmetry, and administrative burden (Table 6.2). Most veteran transition programs predominantly fall into the contract and service P3 typologies. Our research suggests that contract P3s, which are generally time-constrained and have a specific period of performance, are susceptible to principal-agent and informational challenges. In contrast, service P3s, which have extended time horizons, face challenges related to administrative burdens and the establishment of a long-range administrative structure that supports a national veteran employment strategy.

To address these challenges, the federal government should consider a network approach to funding and work collaboratively with P3 ecosystem participants. Instead of creating numerous small grants with undefined or confusing priorities, the government might offer topic-based grants targeting specific veteran transition services, such as employment training, thereby aligning each grant more closely with an actual service function. This approach would enable better measurement of outcomes and more-effective allocation of funds based on clearer prioritization.

Additionally, it is essential to understand both the strengths and limitations of the government's P3 partners. For example, most nonprofits operate with low margins of supplemental funds. If the government intends to use these partners for service delivery, it must clarify its priorities and compensate for these services at a market rate. Otherwise, the P3 organization is left with an underfunded mandate and cannot meet its obligations. Improving informational clarity, structuring funding programs with clear prioritization, and adopting a "whole of government" strategy could significantly help minimize the key challenges of principal-agent dynamics and informational asymmetry.

Longer-term challenges associated with the P3 ecosystem's fiscal stability, persistent government-imposed administrative burdens, and budget monitoring issues are more complex. The government needs information (e.g., performance metrics, such as those described in Chapter 3) to make decisions; however, the process of collecting that information often distorts incentives and shifts resources away from delivering services to administrative activities. Developing improved reporting metrics could help minimize administrative burden.

TABLE 6.2

P3 Challenges by Type, Based on the Extant Literature

Themes	Asset Type	Contract Type	Service Type
Information challenges	Susceptibility to informational asymmetry	Principal-agent challenges, time-constrained performance	Administrative burden, long-term informational needs
Cost challenges	Underfunded mandates for nonprofits	Need for clear prioritization and market rate compensation	Long-term cost of administrative structures
Organization challenges	Structural and administrative burden	Issues with creating short-term objectives that align with long-term goal	Need for coalition building, shared administrative costs

Furthermore, the more the government could support coalitions of nonprofit organizations in conjunction with other funders, the easier it would be for these institutions to share administrative costs and reduce overhead. Many of these long-term alternatives require more research to understand fully. In particular, the fiscal sustainability of the P3 veteran transition and employment ecosystem needs much more research to identify the factors that ensure that grants effectively meet their goals of ensuring that transitioning service members find stable and meaningful employment.

CHAPTER 7

Conclusions and Recommendations

Throughout this report, we sought to describe the current (at the time of writing) and near-future landscape of veteran employment nonprofit organizations by considering different lenses and using a mixed-methods approach. Next, we briefly summarize our findings and present a set of recommendations.

How do leaders in the veteran-serving employment-focused nonprofit community perceive the sustainability of their programs and services, particularly when it comes to future fundraising, collaboration, and measurement of effectiveness?

Service members often need help transitioning from military to veteran life. Nonprofits are an essential part of the "sea of goodwill" providing that support. Most employment- and leadership-focused veteran-serving nonprofits rely on philanthropy from varying combinations of individual, corporate, and foundation donors; government grants and contracts make up a relatively small percentage of revenue overall. Some interviewees expressed concern about their organizations' sustainability in the face of issue competition for charitable giving. Overall, this concern is not supported by survey findings about individual donor propensity to support veterans' causes at the time of writing (although this is not reflective of corporate or foundation giving priorities). Demands for services are expected to increase via referrals from federal transition programs. Unlike in some other sectors, at the time of writing there are limited mechanisms through which organizations may seek federal grants to expand capacity to meet that growing demand.

How do veteran-serving nonprofits measure effectiveness?

All organizations interviewed collect and report data of some kind and consider this an important way to demonstrate the value of their programs; however, inconsistencies in measures complicate comparisons across organizations. Data are typically collected from program administrative data and from surveys of program participants; few indicate using more-formal program evaluation methods, such as random assignment to various programs, comparisons with matched nonparticipants, or pre-/post-treatment designs. Many of the metrics used reflect program inputs and/or outputs rather than outcomes; for example, measuring participation and satisfaction versus securing a job or job details, such as starting salary. Thus, programs report on program activities but often stop short of directly measuring program impacts.

What is the financial landscape of nonprofit organizations supporting veteran transition today, and how is it changing?

Overall, revenue for many veteran-serving nonprofits grew more than revenue for the broader nonprofit sector over the six-year period examined. This trend does not fully support concerns raised during interviews about sector sustainability. However, specific organizations are not assured survival; while giving overall has continued to increase, individual organizations have seen substantial—in some cases, dramatic—declines in revenue. This is particularly true for traditional 501(c)19 VSOs, which can lobby for legislation that could benefit veterans, such as appropriations for new grant-making programs for employment-focused veteran serving nonprofits. Veteran-serving nonprofits focused on employment are more likely to be 501(c)3 organizations, limiting their ability to lobby while eliminating membership requirements. Interviews and assessment of the volatility of revenue indicate that smaller organizations may be better served by consolidating to reduce duplication of effort and/or overhead costs. Organizations that are heavily reliant on corporate or foundation grants may benefit from diversifying their revenue streams to include more individual donor support and, when available, government grants.

What are the prospects for future charitable giving to veterans' causes?

Among survey respondents, individual giving to veterans' issues is on par with or exceeds recent areas of public concern, and a large proportion of the sample reported expecting to give more to veterans' causes in the future. However, most givers currently tend to direct only a small proportion of their total charitable giving to support veterans, and charitable giving to veterans' issues is significantly related to the donor's connection to the military, either directly or through other family members. Should this connection decline over the long term, interest in charitable giving to veterans' issues may also decline; an unrelated survey of affluent households also showed that those born after 1981 are much less likely to highlight veterans' issues as important to them (Bank of America, 2023).

How do veteran-serving nonprofits collaborate with government agencies, and what are the challenges with P3s?

The federal government has long collaborated with nonprofit and private-sector organizations through P3s, most often through contract models, in which there is a set time frame and specific outcome to achieve (e.g., place a certain number of veterans in jobs) or service models, in which the government partners with organizations to provide an ongoing service, such as employment training. These arrangements are subject to several types of challenges, including principal-agent dynamics, administrative burden, and information asymmetry. For example, the DoL's ENPP program faces challenges of financial burden and information asymmetry, since P3 organizations supporting placement and information are not directly funded by this program, but the government relies on the P3 organizations to have sufficient resources to place all those who are referred. To ensure the effectiveness of P3s, the government should compensate for these services at a market rate but also collect performance information to ensure program objectives are met.

After considering insights offered by interviewing nonprofit leaders, analyzing tax revenues, surveying the public about charitable giving, and considering options for collaboration with the federal sector, we developed the following overarching conclusions and recommendations.

Veteran-Serving Nonprofit Revenue Appears Strong, but Sustainability May Require Adaptation

While there are limitations to the methodology used to assess veteran-serving nonprofit revenues by analyzing 990s, recent trends in funding for those veteran nonprofits coded as W30s are generally positive. Additionally, the existing method for identifying nonprofits that support veterans likely leads to a serious *undercount* of available resources. A comprehensive landscape analysis of this sector would be beneficial. Among nonprofits dedicated to veteran transition, employment, and leadership development, some appear to be in a strong position when it comes to finances and performance. These programs may be in a good position to meet employer needs for identifying high-performing employees. These larger, stable, and financially secure programs may be in the best position to assist veteran transitions in the long run and may be able to work collaboratively with smaller, novel programs to develop innovative programming.

The public is generally supportive of charitable donations to veterans, and a near-term dramatic decline seems unlikely. Overall, 31 percent of respondents expect to give more to veteran-serving organizations in the future. Individuals whose donations to veteran-serving organizations constitute a relatively small percentage of their total charitable giving appear especially open to increased giving to veterans' issues and may help supplement losses incurred by declines in corporate giving. However, our review of the financials and our interviews with leaders of nonprofit organizations that focus on providing employment support found that most derive less of their funding from individual donations and more from corporate and foundation support, compared with the broader charitable sector.

Recommendations

- The IRS should improve consistency of NTEE code usage to facilitate future research.
- Smaller nonprofits and those with multiple posts may consider options for increasing sustainability, such as exploring the possibility of consolidation to reduce duplication and increase efficiencies. Given the overhead and administrative burdens involved with any organization, having many small programs with limited evidence of effectiveness dilutes the resources available to serve veterans.
- Given strong public support for veteran-focused philanthropy, employment-focused nonprofits in this sector could consider direct appeals to the public to increase revenue and to diversify revenue streams.

- Nonprofits wishing to appeal to individual donors should consider seeking or improving ratings from independent validators of quality and reliability, such as accreditation by the Better Business Bureau or high ratings on charity-ranking websites.

Identifying High-Performing Organizations Requires Improvements in Measurement and Reporting

Comparing the efficacy of veteran-serving nonprofits is extremely difficult because at the time of writing, nonprofits do not report common or easily comparable measures. Beyond the issue of common measures, veteran-serving nonprofits likely serve different subpopulations; without knowing more about the composition of those served by specific programs (i.e., whether the program serves high-risk populations, general populations of veterans, or more-privileged groups), it can be difficult to make sense of varied levels of success across programs.

Recommendations

- Federal agencies working with employment-focused veteran-serving nonprofits, including DoL, DoD, and VA, should require that they report on a common set of program process and outcome evaluation metrics in a standardized way to increase transparency and accountability (e.g., number of program participants, employment status six months after program completion).
  - This requirement should apply to any organization that signs an agreement with a federal agency related to supporting veteran employment.
  - Consensus should be reached on what measures to include and how to define them by first seeking input from existing DoL and VA federal advisory committees and then publishing proposed measures to transparently solicit public comment.
  - As discussed below, government grants should be developed or modified in a manner that would offset the added costs associated with this requirement.
- Corporate and foundation donors should encourage further transparency and accountability by requiring other grantees to publicize data using the same metrics.
- An independent entity, such as an academic or research organization, should develop a definition of a high-quality veteran employment organization. Once developed, criteria for high-quality and effective organizations can be used to identify high-performing organizations.

Public-Private Partnerships May Be an Opportunity to Enhance P3 Ecosystem Sustainability but Need to Address Partnership and Information Challenges

The P3 ecosystem plays an essential role in ensuring that service members transitioning from the military can successfully move to civilian life. However, the way these partnerships are funded, informed, and prioritized affects their delivery. There may be ways to enhance some of these relationships to improve support for transitioning service members and the employment-focused veteran-serving nonprofit sector more broadly.

Recommendations

- **Address information challenges:** The government should seek ways to be much clearer about its goals and priorities.
  - This involves being more transparent and upfront about requirements, administrative overhead, and decision criteria for grants, which should be clearly articulated in the rulemaking process to improve information resolution, accountability, and alignment with the P3 ecosystem.
  - These criteria should be included in the rulemaking process and should seek to improve transparency by better signaling to the P3 ecosystem.
- **Address cost challenges:** The government should appropriately fund its partners based on its clearly stated goals and carefully consider whether a lack of transparency is creating issues with underfunding or unfunded mandates.
  - Properly account for the value being provided by the partnerships by creating incentives for meeting the terms of contract or service agreements.
  - Ensure that the incentives are designed to be issued at a market rate such that the P3 partner can sustain the program.
  - Develop consistent measures for understanding the P3 ecosystem's financial stability so that grants are more easily able to target gaps in the veteran employment and transition enterprise.
- **Address fiscal sustainability and administrative burden:** Federal agencies should consider a long-term strategy using a "whole of government" approach to support P3 programs for transitioning service members and veterans. This strategy should:
  - implement flexible, per-client grants that include service eligibility and reporting costs, allowing transitioning service members to access and transfer funds between P3 providers, fostering competition and aligning services with demand.
  - use government-covered training models, form administrative coalitions to reduce costs, require staff credentials, and develop cost-sharing tools and a unified data strategy to improve transparency and reduce transaction costs.

Limitations

Maintaining a sharp focus on employment-centered veteran-serving nonprofits provides important insights into the overall ecosystem supporting transitioning service members. In addition, a holistic assessment of overall well-being may offer a more comprehensive framework for assessing successful transitions than an exclusive focus on employment (Karre et al., 2024). Notably, approximately half of veterans enroll in school after leaving the military; 36 percent of post-9/11 veterans enrolled full time (Parker et al., 2019). These veterans may delay their employment searches until they have completed a degree or certification program; at that point, they may be more likely to use search strategies that do not target transitioning service members, including university career service offices.

University career offices are not the only piece of the puzzle that may be inadequately accounted for in analyses of the veteran support ecosystem. The HOH *Veterans in the Workplace* (2023) report shows that 83.3 percent of veterans look for job listings and/or apply for jobs at online job sites and job boards, while only 46.7 percent go to job fairs (and less for every other method). While this report on the employment-focused veteran-serving nonprofit sector and its companion report on the federal sector (Kleykamp et al., 2024) provide valuable context to resources available to transitioning service members, there remain additional segments that are not yet fully explored, including corporate, state, and local programs and resources.

An additional caveat is needed when considering what our findings may mean for the future: All are premised on an assumption that certain underlying trends, such as the number of service members transitioning annually and the type of economy into which they transition, will remain relatively static. Should the United States enter a major conflict that dramatically increases the number of transitioning service members, the ability of existing services to serve them may be overwhelmed. Additionally, a major macroeconomic change, such as a major recession, could dramatically change employment prospects for veterans and nonveterans alike, with unknown outcomes (Schwam and Marrone, 2023).

Surveys asking about willingness to contribute to veteran charities have the potential to elicit overly positive responses because of social desirability in responding to questions about veterans (Kleykamp, Hipes, and MacLean, 2018), which may have influenced ALP responses.

Finally, our data on the financial landscape of veteran-serving nonprofits (i.e., revenue among organizations in this sector) should be interpreted in light of methodological challenges. RAND researchers followed past approaches to finding and analyzing these data from available sources but found they were limited in what information they offered. Current reporting practices are insufficient to generate consistent and reliable financial data across different organizations operating to serve veterans. And there are limitations in the available methods to assess the size and revenue trends of these organizations using IRS tax data and financial statements, including but not limited to taxonomy inconsistencies. The W30 designation can be one tool used to broadly assess trends in the revenue and expenses of veteran-serving nonprofits, but it is imperfect and imprecise, given that it may not be used by nonprofits that serve a substantial number of veterans and may also be used by nonprofits that do not. A strength of this approach, as a replication of methodology used in prior reports, is that it allows the monitoring of trends in revenue through time.

Conclusion

Nonprofit organizations play a significant role in the ecosystem of support for service members during their transition to veteran status and the civilian job market; their efforts have likely contributed to veterans having lower unemployment rates than nonveterans for several years. Despite concerns among some advocates and organization leaders about the financial sustainability of these organizations in a shifting environment with less public visibility for veterans' issues and other issues competing for philanthropic resources, overall, recent trends in revenue and public opinion about philanthropic donations for this sector were strong. P3s could diversify funding streams and increase long-term sustainability among organizations the government relies on for services, although the federal government needs to fund these partnerships appropriately and seek ways to reduce information asymmetry and financial and administrative burdens.

The level of innovation and experimentation possible within the private sector may not be replicable or sustainable within the public sector. Enhanced government support could be designed thoughtfully to increase transparency, accountability, and sustainable financing of private-sector efforts while maintaining their nimbleness, allowing rapid response to changing conditions in the future.

APPENDIX A

Interview Participants

The following 14 organizations consented to be acknowledged as interview participants. We greatly appreciate their contributions to this research.

- American Corporate Partners
- The American Legion
- Black Veterans for Social Justice
- Bob Woodruff Foundation
- Combined Arms
- ETS Sponsorship
- Hire Heroes USA
- Hiring Our Heroes
- D'Aniello Institute for Veterans and Military Families at Syracuse University
- Military Family Research Institute at Purdue University
- The Mission Continues
- Travis Manion Foundation
- VetJobs
- Wounded Warrior Project

APPENDIX B

Interview Codes

TABLE B.1
Interview Codes

ID	Parent ID	Title	Description
1	1	A. Organization's characteristics	How does the participant describe their organization's program (i.e., how it operates, how it serves transitioning service members, veterans and/or their families)?
2	1	A.1 Why the veteran population?	Why did the participant choose to invest in veterans?
3	2	B. Organization's successes	What is working well in their organization?
4	2	B.1 Reasons for successes & examples	Why does the participant think their organization is working well? Any examples provided?
5	3	C. Organization's struggles	What does the participant describe as struggles that their organization is facing?
6	3	C.1 Reasons for struggles & examples	Why does the participant think their organization is struggling? How do they know? Any examples provided?
7	3	C.2 Attempts to solve organization's struggles	Have they tried anything to solve their issues? Has the participant or others in the organization moved away from these practices because they didn't work?
8	4	D. Formal evaluations	Do they conduct any formal evaluations? If so, how do they do it?
9	4	D.1 Inputs, outputs, or outcomes	Do they use inputs, outputs, or try to get to outcomes? If they don't use outcomes, why not?
10	5	E. Additional programs	Do they work with additional programs regularly that also serve their target population?
11	5	E.1 Reasons	Why do these hand-offs or relationships exist?
12	5	E.2 Transfers & causes	What leads to passing a client on to another organization or receiving a client from another?
13	6	F. Federal transition programs–organizational activity	How does the participant characterize their relationship with federal transition programs?
14	6	F.1 Clients: transferred-in	Do they "receive" clients that have already used federal transition services? Which ones?

Table B.1—Continued

ID	Parent ID	Title	Description
15	6	F.2 Reasons	Why does the participant think this happens?
16	6	F.3 Clients: transferred-out	Does the participant send individuals to other federal programs? Why and which ones?
17	6	F.4 Relationship comments	Additional comments on their relationship with federal transition programs, how they pick who to partner with, etc.?
18	7	G. Federal transition programs	How does the participant feel the federal transition programs are performing?
19	7	G.1 Federal transition programs–relationship	What is the participant's relationship to these programs?
20	8	H. Transition assistance	Given the many federal transition programs, why does the participant think there is a robust nongovernmental/ philanthropic effort dedicated to transition? [Probes/ examples: accessibility? Effectiveness? Community-based/ local versus national? Subgroup focused (age, rank, demographics, others)?]
21	9	I. Finances	How does the participant's organization finance work?
22	9	I.1 Finances' evolution	How has the funding model/sources changed over time?
23	10	J. Funding	What challenges does the participant face in funding their programs?
24	10	J.1 Funding's evolution	How have the challenges changed over time?
25	10	J.2 Competition	Is there any competition among other veteran-serving nongovernment programs?
26	10	J.3 Others	What other issues/areas/populations does the participant perceive to be competing for funds?
27	10	J.4 Impact	What does the participant foresee as impacts if funding were to decrease?
28	10	J.5 Various	Various comments on funding that do not fall in J.1–J.4
29	11	K. Program sustainability	What concerns does the participant have about the future sustainability of their program?
30	11	K.1 Program's future changes	Does the participant's organization have any novel funding streams or funding models to be sustainable into the future?
31	12	L. Looking into the future	What does the participant think the future of the veteran-serving nongovernment space looks like?
32	12	L.1 Participant's role	How does the participant see their position in this space in the future?
33	13	M. Additional comments/ recommendations	Any additional comments/recommendations that the participant mentioned
34	13	M.1 Thoughts/comments	Additional thoughts/comments
35	13	M.2 Specific recommendations	Specific recommendations

APPENDIX C

Additional Interview Findings

Meredith Kleykamp and Kayla M. Williams

We asked organizations about their relationship with federal transition programs and services to better understand the overlap in services and any gaps and needs unmet by federal programs. Some organizations commented on DoD's TAP, often critically. These perspectives included the following:

Lack of program outcome data. Some respondents questioned what TAP achieves and noted its lack of outcome evaluations. As one person put it, "I don't know because I have not seen any outcome data. That is problematic given all the money spent and lack of outcomes. Should raise some eyebrows." Another went farther on this point, noting that both the federal entities overseeing and the organizations contracted to implement the TAP curriculum seem disconnected from the nongovernment organizations (like theirs) that do collect data and evaluate the effectiveness of their programs. The lack of visibility of the federal program representatives or the contractor representatives was seen as very dysfunctional. The nonprofit program representatives we spoke to work with the very people TAP produces (or fails to produce), and they had unique insights into what may be functioning better and worse in the program based on the clients they serve who have gone through TAP.

Lack of sufficient nuance and specialization. Some organization leaders perceived that the "one size fits all" approach of TAP limits its effectiveness, given the extremely diverse set of people transitioning out of the military every year. The different TAP tracks (employment, education, and entrepreneurship) presume that the transitioning service members know the right track to pursue when, in fact, what they may need is coaching and guidance on what is likely the right track for them—services that nonprofit programs say they can provide more effectively and efficiently.

Simply too large, complex, or inconsistent. Some representatives noted that the TAP program has so many components, from the VA, DoL, and DoD to the learning materials on benefits and additional resources, that it is challenging for participants to absorb and collaborators to keep track of to understand where supplemental support may be needed. Additionally, the curriculum is implemented by different people across each installation, with anecdotal evidence that contract employee experience varies tremendously by site. Some noted that their organization may or may not have been on the list of additional resources provided to those going through TAP, and it was very dependent on local relationships whether specific nonprofit programs would or would not be highlighted. While TAP officials may not want to be seen as endorsing or advocating one nongovernmental program over another, at the site level, instructors or leaders may be providing such information based on their personal relationships or perspectives or local connections. There is no list of vetted nonprofit programs or recommended programs, leaving transitioning service members to navigate program selection on their own.

Federal programs are doing what they can. Not all leaders felt that federal programs were doing a bad job. Some were not critical of federal programs overall or TAP specifically. These interviewees acknowledged that perhaps DoD isn't responsible for ensuring a postservice job to those who leave, or that there are limits to what a near-universal three-to-five-day program can do. As noted by one participant, "People say TAP sucks; that's not fair. TAP has a specific goal, and they achieve it, but that goal is not to get everyone a job." Another offered this insight:

> DoD's job is to win wars, and it's not their job to transition people into successful veterans. The job to help veterans transition is best left to philanthropy. They do it better than government. Having VA be a warm handoff, and making information available to veterans, is their appropriate role.

Both ideas may in fact be true. However, suggesting that government has no real obligation to help transitioning service members find jobs after military service is likely a difficult position to take in the current cultural and political climate. Moreover, as some organizational leaders noted, leaving it entirely up to philanthropy means veteran employment programs would be subject to the ups and downs of private fundraising.

Needed: attention to the cultural and identity-related challenge faced by veterans. Finally, one topic that some representatives felt TAP or a different federal program should tackle is the cultural and identity-related transitions that come along with leaving the military. As one representative put it,

> You know, you spend so much time institutionalizing people to military service and getting them into the culture to do the hard work that mission requires, and even up into fighting the nation's wars, and engaging in direct combat requires that boot camp, crucible experience to get people bonded in that way and understanding that mission. I guess the line for me is what ethical responsibility then as leaders [we have] . . . to say now, how do we deinstitutionalize or prepare them for that next level [civilian life], and that's where I think the biggest miss is, quite honestly.

Another similarly said,

> You've got to think about what purpose you fulfill in this place, and I would say extending that [pre-separation transition] timeline a little bit. Because the tangible things of writing a résumé, or whatever, all hinge on the person's capability to understand themselves and where they fit in this broader culture. That's the biggest miss of TAP I think.

For these representatives and others, what TAP doesn't provide is a more holistic approach to understanding the reverse socialization that transition involves when returning to civilian life.

APPENDIX D

Tools for Program Management, Planning, and Evaluation

Jennie W. Wenger

In this appendix, we introduce several tools that can play important roles in program management, planning, and evaluation. We provide specific examples of how these tools can assist programs. We begin by providing background on logic models.

A *logic model*, which can be thought of as a road map to guide a program, is a useful tool for defining and clarifying a program's structure, activities, and expected results. Logic models are especially helpful to illustrate and identify the specific outcomes that would be expected from a given program and to link program activities to these eventual outcomes. By offering such a linkage, a logic model can serve as a key tool to help determine the effectiveness of a given program. Finally, logic models can be helpful communication devices to ensure that funders, program staff, and other stakeholders have a common vision of a program.[1]

As a demonstration of how logic models can be used, we provide a specific example of a logic model for a youth program. While the National Guard Youth Challenge (ChalleNGe) program serves a different population from veteran-serving programs, ChalleNGe does provide some services that are similar to those provided by many veteran-serving nonprofits. Therefore, the program's logic model serves as a relevant example. ChalleNGe uses a *whole person* model; thus, the program provides a variety of services to participants and is designed to influence a broad variety of outcomes. This aspect of the program means that various aspects of the logic model may be relevant to different veteran-serving programs. First, we provide a brief description of ChalleNGe; next, we walk through the key sections of the program logic model. Finally, we discuss how the ChalleNGe logic model has influenced our approach to determining program effectiveness.

The ChalleNGe program is a quasi-military residential program for young people who struggle in traditional high schools. The program is 22 weeks in length; during this time,

---

[1] Helpful guidance for developing and working with logic models is found in Knowlton and Phillips (2009). Note that a theory of change can serve a similar role, although this tool generally puts less emphasis on specific outcome measures. For more information about this tool, see (among many) Funnell and Rogers (2011).

participants (generally referred to as *cadets*) dress in a uniform manner and often live in barracks-style housing. Cadets spend substantial time on classroom work; they also take part in physical fitness activities and perform community service. The program focuses on eight core components: academic excellence, leadership/followership, responsible citizenship, service to community, life-coping skills, physical fitness, health and hygiene, and job skills. Thus, the program provides a variety of different services to cadets. As of this writing, the program has 39 sites in 28 states, the District of Columbia, and Puerto Rico. The mission of the program is to "intervene in and reclaim the lives of 16–18 year old high school dropouts, producing program graduates with the values, life skills, education, and self-discipline necessary to succeed as productive citizens" (National Guard Youth ChalleNGe, undated).

RAND researchers have worked closely with program leadership and staff over the past decade ("National Guard ChalleNGe Project," undated). As part of these efforts, the RAND team developed a logic model to describe ChalleNGe; this model, which has been refined over time, appears in Figure D.1.

Logic models serve to describe the ways in which a program's structure and activities could be expected to generate intended outcomes. Logic models typically include four main categories: *inputs*, *activities*, *outputs*, and *outcomes*. Inputs are the program's assets or resources; as shown in Figure D.1, these can include staff, facilities, funding, and volunteers, as well as policy and planning resources. *Activities*, which can be divided by program phase, as is the case in Figure D.1, include the specific services or activities that make up the program. *Outputs* describe the expected immediate results or products that occur within the program. Finally, *outcomes* (which can be divided by time frame, as is the case in Figure D.1), describe the changes that are expected to occur as a result of the program. In the case of ChalleNGe, outcomes are broad in nature and reflective of the program's mission. But for virtually any program, a logic model can demonstrate or document the change that is expected (Wenger, Constant, and Cottrell, 2018).

An effective program with a careful logic model is expected to produce the specific outcomes expressed in the program's logic model. In other words, participants who take part in an effective program would be expected to have *different* outcomes than otherwise similar individuals who did not take part in this program. This implies that programs should seek to measure these outcomes. However, measuring long-term (or even medium-term) outcomes is a complex endeavor. Again, we use the ChalleNGe program to demonstrate several relevant points.

Researchers have studied ChalleNGe extensively since the program's founding in the mid-1990s, and, unlike many programs, ChalleNGe has undergone formal evaluation. The evaluation demonstrated that the program is *effective*—those who complete ChalleNGe have higher levels of educational attainment and earnings than similar young people who do not

FIGURE D.1
Example Logic Model

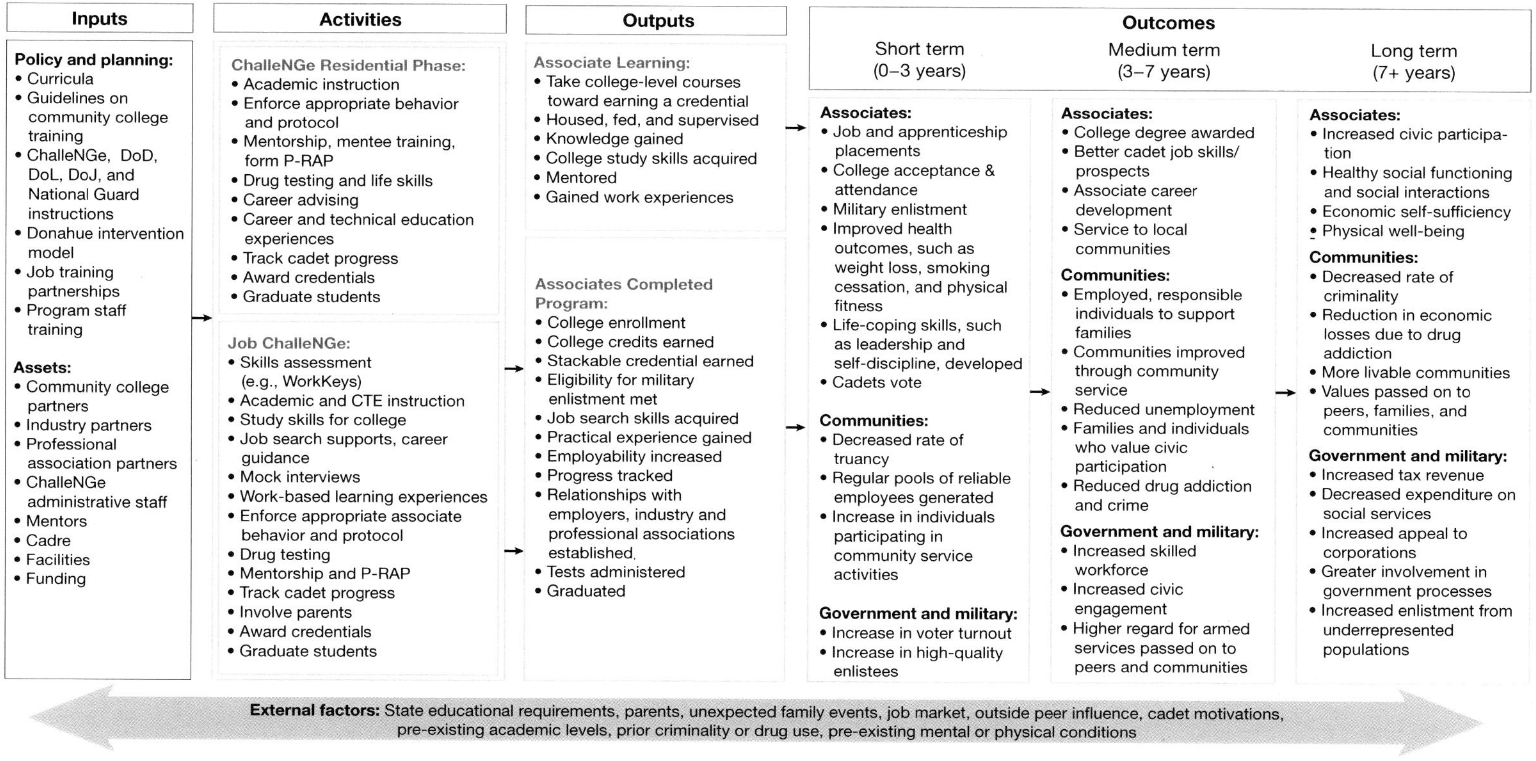

SOURCE: Reproduced from Wenger, Constant, and Cottrell, 2018.

attend ChalleNGe (Millenky et al., 2011).[2] Additionally, ChalleNGe is *cost-effective*; the benefit to society is substantially larger than the cost of the program (Perez-Arce et al., 2012).[3]

This type of formal evaluation is typically carried out for large programs with long histories; such an approach is neither appropriate nor practical for smaller programs with shorter histories. However, the *ideas* behind such evaluation offer value to most programs. In short, accurately measuring program outcomes requires some estimate of what would have happened in the absence of the program.

A practical, cost-effective way to understand a program's effects is through *benchmarking*. Benchmarking is commonly thought of as comparing outcomes from a given program with an external standard; in the case of a veteran-serving program, benchmarking would require an existing and accepted standard. Alternatively, programs can benchmark outcomes of individual participants against standards derived from similar individuals who were not served by the program. This type of benchmarking requires available data or measures on similar populations, but it can be quite effective and efficient. Returning again to the ChalleNGe program, benchmarks from publicly available data sources can be used to get a rough sense of the outcomes that might be expected in the absence of ChalleNGe; such analyses reveal that joblessness is substantially higher among those who leave high school without a diploma.[4] These figures and similar figures for other relevant outcomes can serve to contextualize outcome measures for program staff and stakeholders.

To summarize, logic models and benchmarks both have the potential to play key roles in determining program effectiveness, and this is possible without making substantial investments (in money and time) to carry out a formal evaluation.

---

2 Program effectiveness was demonstrated through a randomized control trial (RCT). RCTs are considered the gold standard for program evaluation, but the process is expensive, requires a substantial amount of time, and is not without criticism (e.g., Deaton and Cartwright, 2018). RCTs are most common among large, federally funded programs; in addition to ChalleNGe, both Job Corps and the Job Training Partnership Act programs have been evaluated.

3 This is based on a cost-benefit analysis using the results of Millenky et al. (2011).

4 For example, national data indicate that 32 to 40 percent of nongraduates aged 19 to 29 did not have a job during the previous year (Edwards, 2020).

APPENDIX E

NTEE Codes

Following are the NTEE code descriptions from organizations listed in Table 4.4 in alphabetical and numeric order (Urban Institute, 2019).

- F30: Mental Health Treatment
- J20: Employment Preparation & Procurement
- J21: Vocational Counseling
- J22: Job Training
- O50: Youth Development Programs
- P20: Human Service Organizations
- S41: Chambers of Commerce & Business Leagues
- S50: Nonprofit Management
- S99: Community Improvement & Capacity Building

APPENDIX F

IRS Designations for Veteran-Serving Nonprofit Organizations

Kayla M. Williams and Shaddy K. Saba

There are many types of tax-exempt organizations, including traditional charitable organizations, churches and religious organizations, and private foundations. The organizational requirements of each type can dictate opportunities for funding and the activities organizations can engage in. Among all nonprofits, 72 percent are recognized under Internal Revenue Code Section as 501(c)(3) public charities; generally, these organizations may not attempt to influence legislation and may receive tax-deductible contributions (Koob, 2021).

A substantial majority of W30 organizations, however, are recognized under 501(c)(19), which applies only to veterans' organizations and their auxiliaries. The IRS notes that these organizations "occupy a special place in the world of exempt organizations":

> Not only are most veterans' organizations exempt from tax, contributions to them may be deductible, and some are permitted to set aside amounts that are used to provide insurance benefits for members. This combination—tax-exempt status, deductibility of contributions and the ability to pay benefits to members—is relatively rare and is evidence of Congress' intent to provide special tax treatment for veterans' organizations. When coupled with the ability to engage in both lobbying activities and political activities, it is fair to say that veterans' organizations are unique in the tax-exempt sector. (IRS, 2018)

This special status also involves stricter requirements than many other tax-exempt entities, however. At least 75 percent of members must be past or present members of the U.S. Armed Forces, and at least 97.5 percent of members must be present or former members of the U.S. Armed Forces, cadets, or their spouses or survivors (IRS, 2018). Most 501(c)(19) veterans' organizations are part of a group exemption letter, in which a central or headquarters organization supervises or controls subordinate organizations or posts that share its uniform governing instruments; they may also have associated auxiliaries, trusts, or foundations. Posts are also able to offer recreational and social activities, including gambling and dining, to members and their invited guests tax-free (IRS, 2018).

> The ability of VSOs organized under IRS section 501(c)19 to engage in both lobbying and political activities while maintaining tax-exempt status and deductibility of contributions is unique among not-for-profit organizations.

There are several other sections under which veterans' organizations can be granted tax-exempt status, including 501(c)(4) social welfare organizations, 501(c)(7) social clubs, 501(c)(8) and 501(c)(10) fraternal organizations, and two veterans' organizations established prior to 1880 that are recognized under 501(c)(23); together these make up 11 percent of W30 organizations (IRS, 2023c). Seventeen percent are recognized under 501(c)(3) as public charities.

Of the subset of W30 organizations we categorized as having an employment focus, nearly 80 percent were recognized as 501(c)(3) public charities, 16 percent as 501(c)(19) veterans' organizations, and 5 percent as "other." This breakdown aligns more closely with the broader nonprofit sector. Notably, compared with 501(c)(19)s, 501(c)(3) organizations simultaneously face restrictions on their ability to lobby for legislative changes that could benefit those they serve and are not required to maintain a majority-veteran membership base.

The W30 Classification Does Not Capture the Breadth of Veteran Organizations

To explore whether the W30 NTEE code accurately captures organizations in the veteran-serving nonprofit sector, we checked whether organizations known to serve veterans in a specific geographic region were nonprofit organizations in the GuideStar database classified with the W30 NTEE code. PAServes Greater Pittsburgh, described in the box below, operates in Southwestern Pennsylvania. The Heinz Endowments provided a list of all entities that referred to or received at least one referral from PAServes in the 12 months preceding June 2023. We determined that 73.6 percent of those PAServes participating organizations

About PAServes of Greater Pittsburgh

The PAServes of Greater Pittsburgh program is designed to help service members, veterans, and their families connect with resources in Pennsylvania's Allegheny, Butler, and Westmoreland counties. It was founded in 2015 with a grant from The Heinz Endowments (which also supported this research) as part of the national AmericaServes network run by Syracuse University's D'Aniello Institute for Veterans and Military Families (Syracuse University, undated-b).

PAServes staff and participating service providers use a shared technology platform to coordinate access to resources across a range of topic areas. These include "education, health care, employment, housing, human services, legal, social activities, mentoring, sports and fitness, and community engagement." This diverse expertise results in improved time fulfilling service requests (Roller, 2020).

are nonprofit organizations (or housed within nonprofit organizations), the remainder being for-profit health services, financial institutions, or government entities. Of these nonprofit organizations in the PAServes network, only 20.5 percent (or 15.1 percent of all participating organizations) are classified under the W30 NTEE code.

This analysis suggests that the W30 classification does not fully capture the breadth of nonprofit organizations serving veterans, at least in this geographic region. This is likely in part because many organizations that serve veterans do so as part of a broader mission (e.g., health care, homelessness) and provide services to broader populations in need of these services (i.e., nonveterans). In other words, there are many organizations that are not strictly "military and veteran organizations" that are actively providing services to veterans, which poses a challenge in terms of assessing the financial landscape of the veteran-serving sector.[1] Even some of the largest (by revenue and expenses) and most-respected organizations that are explicitly focused on providing employment-related services to veterans, such as HOH and Hire Heroes USA, do not use the W30 code.

---

[1] Additionally, not all organizations that select the W30 designation appear to include veterans' issues in their mission or population served, such as the Seminar Network (as noted in Table 4.1).

APPENDIX G

American Life Panel Survey Supplement

R. Gordon Rinderknecht and Meredith Kleykamp

Figure G.1 highlights the broad distribution of all charitable giving that goes to veterans' issues among the 14 percent of respondents who donate to veteran-serving charities. Just over half of these respondents gave less than 25 percent of their total donations to veterans' issues (185 respondents in total) relative to those who gave 25 percent or more (148 respondents in total).

FIGURE G.1

Proportion of All Giving That Goes to Veterans' Issues Among Those Who Give to Veterans' Issues

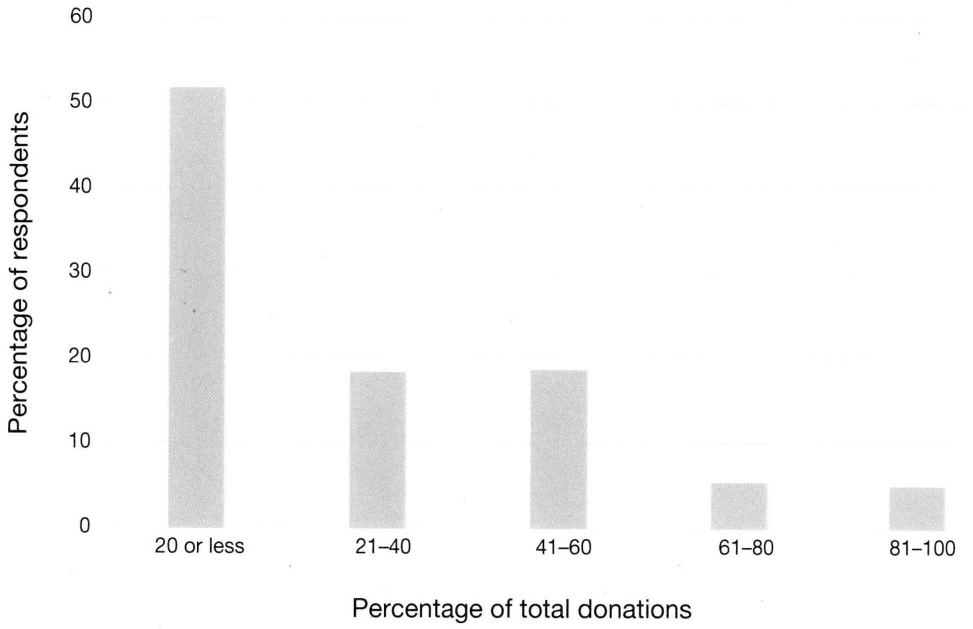

SOURCE: Features data from ALP #615 (2023). *N* = 333.
NOTE: All estimates are weighted.

Figure G.2 highlights the broad distribution of money donated by respondents across our sample. Figure G.3 expands on Figure 5.6 by separating the respondents who do not give to veterans' issues but donate $1,000 or more per year to other causes (388 respondents in total) from others who do not donate to veterans' issues (1,171 respondents in total). Relative to other giving categories, those donating $1,000 or more exclusively to nonveteran causes stand out because of the importance they place on their connection to charitable organizations and the lack of importance they place on direct solicitation. Although these high-value givers may be a potential source of future support for veterans' issues, the low importance of advertisements combined with the relative ineffectiveness of direct solicitation makes this group uniquely challenging to reach.

Table G.1 provides an overview of the demographic background of both our analytic sample (*orig.*) and the subsample of respondents who had data for our supplemental variables merged from earlier ALP waves (*sup.*). Those who donate to support veterans' issues differ demographically from those who do not donate to veterans' issues. When reading this table, note that bold numbers indicate that the demographic factor (e.g., race) was a statistically significant factor in distinguishing between our three giving categories. Overall, in the analytic sample, respondents who donate to veterans' issues are disproportionately White (non-

FIGURE G.2
Proportion of Respondents Who Donate Each Dollar Amount

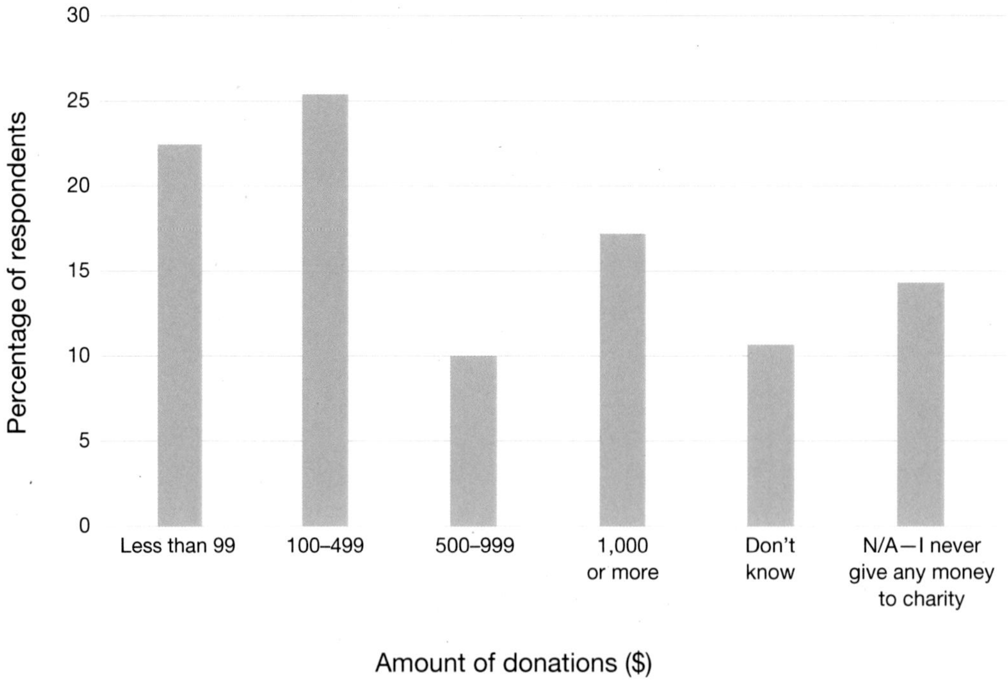

SOURCE: Features data from ALP #615 (2023). *N* = 1,892.
NOTE: All estimates are weighted.

FIGURE G.3

Most Important Factors Affecting Respondents' Charitable Giving Decisions, by Expanded Giving Categories

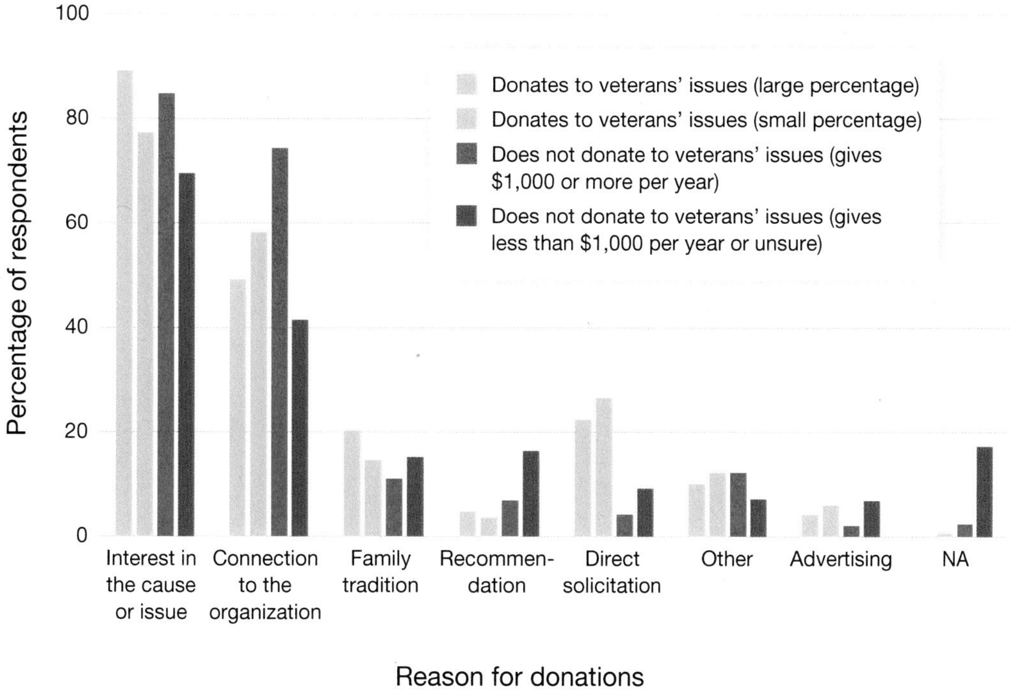

SOURCE: Features data from ALP #615 (2023). N = 1,892.

NOTE: All estimates are weighted. Respondents reported their top two choices. The non–veteran-giving, high-value group places significantly more importance on connection to the organization relative to other nonveteran givers and those who give a large percentage of their total giving to veterans' issues. The non–veteran-giving, high-value group also places significantly less importance on direct solicitation than all other giving categories. Respondents who give nothing to veterans' issues and give less than $1,000 per year in charitable giving were more likely to select NA, indicating they give nothing to charity, and more likely to report relying on recommendations relative to other giving categories. These non–veteran-giving respondents are also less likely to report interest in the cause relative to those who donate a large percentage of their giving to veterans' issues and relative to nonveteran, high-value givers. *Significance* refers to statistical significance in a logistic regression with respondents' selection of each issue as the dependent variable and giving category as the independent variable.

Hispanic) or American Indian, Alaska Native, Asian, or Pacific Islander (AI/AN/Asian/PI) (non-Hispanic), generally higher income, and more likely to live outside the Western United States relative to those who donate nothing to veterans' issues. Forty-four percent of respondents in our analytical sample had responses for all supplemental variables. This subgroup differed from the full analytic sample in notable ways. Giving categories in the supplemental sample also differed in terms of race, but not income or region. Instead, the supplemental sample differed in terms of gender, with those donating a large percentage of their total giving to veterans' issues being disproportionately male.

There are significant differences between giving categories for all supplementary variables. Specifically, giving to veterans' issues associates with being a Republican, agreement

TABLE G.1

Demographic Overview and Supplemental Measures (%)

	Donates to Veteran Issues (Large %)		Donates to Veteran Issues (Small %)		Does Not Donate to Veteran Issues	
	Sup.	**Orig.**	**Sup.**	**Orig.**	**Sup.**	**Orig.**
N	69	148	81	185	676	1,559
Age						
18–24	—	0	—	0	—	9
25–34	0	0	6	22	7	21
35–44	20	19	5	12	15	18
45–54	8	19	7	11	24	16
55–64	23	22	19	13	22	16
65–74	34	25	30	26	23	14
75+	15	14	32	16	10	6
Gender						
Male	**71**	55	**49**	58	**46**	47
Female	**29**	45	**51**	42	**54**	53
Race						
White, non-Hispanic	**89**	**85**	**91**	**73**	**63**	**61**
Black/African American, non-Hispanic	**3**	**3**	**4**	**4**	**8**	**13**
Hispanic	**4**	**8**	**4**	**5**	**19**	**17**
AI/AN/Asian/PI, non-Hispanic	**1**	**2**	**1**	**18**	**5**	**5**
Other, non-Hispanic	**2**	**2**	**0**	**0**	**4**	**4**
Marital status						
Married or living with a partner	64	72	68	53	60	57
Separated	0	0	3	1	2	1
Divorced	23	13	15	9	13	10
Widowed	8	7	11	6	8	5
Single (never married)	6	7	4	31	17	27
Educational attainment						
Less than high school	0	3	6	2	7	9
High school (or equivalent)	50	42	17	22	36	30
Some college/associate's	30	31	36	42	24	24

Table G.1—Continued

	Donates to Veteran Issues (large %)		Donates to Veteran Issues (small %)		Does Not Donate to Veteran Issues	
	Sup.	Orig.	Sup.	Orig.	Sup.	Orig.
Bachelor's	9	12	15	18	19	20
Master's+	11	12	26	17	15	17
Employment status						
Yes	56	59	36	54	56	62
No	44	41	64	46	44	38
Household income						
$0–$9,999	0	**0**	0	**7**	8	**6**
$10,000–$24,999	10	**6**	9	**6**	12	**8**
$25,000–$49,999	13	**14**	12	**12**	22	**20**
$50,000–$99,999	44	**28**	35	**24**	29	**33**
$100,000+	33	**51**	44	**51**	30	**33**
Household size						
1–2 members	56	44	73	57	60	50
3–4 members	24	37	22	21	29	37
5+ members	20	19	5	21	11	13
Urban or rural						
Urban	52	69	67	75	74	77
Rural	48	31	33	25	26	23
Region						
North	30	**28**	16	**21**	17	**19**
South	35	**29**	36	**27**	42	**43**
Midwest	22	**25**	25	**37**	14	**15**
West	14	**18**	23	**15**	27	**23**
Political affiliation						
Republican	**56**	—	**45**	—	**24**	—
Democrat	**15**	—	**22**	—	**37**	—
Independent	**23**	—	**23**	—	**23**	—
Other	**2**	—	**4**	—	**4**	—
Not sure	**4**	—	**8**	—	**12**	—

Table G.1—Continued

	Donates to Veteran Issues (large %)		Donates to Veteran Issues (small %)		Does Not Donate to Veteran Issues	
	Sup.	Orig.	Sup.	Orig.	Sup.	Orig.
Veteran stereotypes "Veterans are more reliable and hard-working than the rest of society"						
Strongly agree	**20**	—	**28**	—	**12**	—
Agree	**72**	—	**63**	—	**55**	—
Disagree	**5**	—	**9**	—	**30**	—
Strongly disagree	**4**	—	**0**	—	**3**	—
Military affiliation						
Family is serving/veteran	**65**	—	**63**	—	**51**	—
Respondent is serving/veteran	**12**	—	**3**	—	**3**	—
Both	**18**	—	**18**	—	**7**	—
Neither	**5**	—	**15**	—	**39**	—

SOURCES: Features data from ALP #615 analytic sample merged with #566 + #546 (political affiliation), #591 (veteran stereotypes), and #574 (military affiliation) (Pollard and Baird, 2017).

NOTE: All estimates are weighted. Sup. = subsection of the analytic sample consisting of respondents with supplemental measures. Orig. = original full analytic sample. Results in bold represent statistically significant differences across categories in their respective datasets (supplemental and original) at $p < 0.05$, based on Pearson's χ^2 test statistic.

with the belief that veterans are more reliable and hard-working than the rest of society, and being in some way affiliated with the military.

APPENDIX H

Evolution of VA's P3 Ecosystem

Brandon F. De Bruhl

In this appendix, we describe how VA's relationship with nonprofit organizations has evolved over time, demonstrating that the P3 ecosystem has been coproduced through a concentrated effort of community pressures, congressional actions, and administrative progressives. VA, as a formal institution, serves an essential role as a tool for solving the large and complex problems faced by the veteran community. The P3 ecosystem allows flexibility for veteran communities, states, and organizations to tailor their services to their local service populations. It calls on VA's federal powers to solve problems beyond the community or state programs' ability to address. This appendix briefly covers the history of the VA P3 ecosystem and contextualizes this history with punctuated equilibrium theory.

The Origins of Veteran Services

By best accounts, VA's P3 ecosystem emerged organically over many years. One history notes that civilian groups have actively supported retired service members since 1776 (Bodenger, 1971). States became essential actors in the post–Civil War period by developing state veteran homes; many are now operating as nonprofits today, and they were intended to serve the most severely injured, such as amputees, or support employment for those who could not participate in the labor market (Kelly, 1997). Before the 20th century, the locus of veteran services predominantly fell to a mixture of state-funded enterprises, business and community initiatives, and individual veteran families, which coproduced a semiformal social network that returning service members could leverage for employment, financial support, and health-related care (Cimbala, 2015). These included the Grand Army of the Republic Organization (c. 1866), Veterans of Foreign Wars (c. 1899), and several social clubs, such as the Aztec Club (c. 1847) (Tucker, 2012; Pencak, 2009).

The latter half of the 19th and the early 20th centuries saw a shift from informal social networks toward increased institutionalization (Burtin, 2020a, 2020b). Several federal institutions were founded: the Interior Department's Bureau of Pensions (1833), the National Home for Disabled Volunteer Soldiers (1866), and the Bureau of War Risk Insurance (1913) (Adler, 2017). These institutions established the administrative precedent, along with some robust campaigns from the Harding administration in 1922, that the government should be responsible for providing centralized veteran services. The fractionalized and complex nature of accessing these informal (community) and formal (state and federal) service networks led to the establishment of the Veterans Bureau in 1922 (Stevens, 2016). While politically and administratively difficult, this transition moved the locus of authority away from the distributed community and state-driven ecosystem to a new centrally administered federal system.

The First Era—Veteran Social Movements and Ad Hoc Services

The early federal system stumbled, and the challenge centered on the jurisdiction of service provision and the interaction of the formal and informal networks. Congress endowed three federal entities to manage the Veteran Affairs Service: (1) the National Soldiers Home, (2) the Pensions Bureau, and (3) the newly formed Veterans Bureau. The Harding administration's objective was to organize services better to allow the influx of returning World War I veterans increased levels of access and support (Ridgway, 2013). These efforts fell short, as increased federal oversight and administrative overhead created further barriers to entry (Burtin, 2020a). In light of the increased federal complexity, the informal community and state systems, such as the American Legion (c. 1919), reemerged as tools for veterans seeking assistance or to access government services (Campbell, 2010).

The increased need for more-robust veteran-focused services and an increase in veterans from World War I mobilized political pressure. The newly elected Hoover administration identified significant challenges to having a tripartite administrative structure, including duplicative services, conflicting requirements, and cost discrepancies (Fausold, 1985). Executive Order 5398 consolidated the three Veteran Services Bureaus into a single Veterans Administrative Agency. At Congress's direction, the President "consolidates and coordinates" the government's activities affecting veteran services (Hoover, 1930). The Great Depression of the 1930s put enormous pressure on the government and civilian actors who provided services to veterans.

The VA's unification reflected the Wilsonian ideals of bureaucratic centralization and the Hoover administration's desire to streamline the expanded federal agencies to lower costs (Burtin, 2020b). As with many administrative agencies established during this period, there was a tendency to move power away from defusing service networks and a technical and obtuse benefits system. While the VA started to consolidate power and administrative acumen, further economic hardships of the era mobilized the veteran social networks to march on Washington (Burtin, 2020a). In 1924, Congress passed the World War I Veterans' Act to ensure that returning service members would receive an enumerated payment as a "bonus" (Huston, 1925). These bonuses were issued as certificates with an almost 20-year delay. The result was that thousands of World War I veterans moved onto the mall and established a "Hooverville" tent camp in protest of the lack of payment. The occupation turned violent, and Hoover directed the U.S. Army to remove the veterans. Again, the veterans mobilized, with many switching their vote to Franklin Delano Roosevelt (FDR) the following November (Wilson, 1974).

Second Era—Veteran Affairs as Federal Social Services

A central element of FDR's administrative plan was quickly responding to the demands of the veteran movements. The passage of the Economy Act of 1933 enabled the President to restructure VA benefit programs and codify the previously ad hoc benefit system into an increasingly centralized administrative state (Ortiz, 2009a). The "New Deal" programs emerged as part of broad social reform; veteran groups feared that increased social services programs for nonveterans would erode the newly gained benefits system and priority of the VA (Ortiz, 2009b). Eventually, Congress overrode the President's veto to protect veteran benefit programs. As in previous administrations, veteran groups coalesced as a social movement to reshape how and when the federal government would provide veteran services (Ortiz, 2009b).

Unsurprisingly, World War II played a large role in expanding the VA's programs and benefits. As with previous expansions, veterans' groups, states, and partnerships were critical in driving administrative change (Hunt and Robbins, 2001). The American Legion proposed and advocated what became the GI Bill's foundation (Altschuler and Blumin, 2009). The FDR administration and Congress both saw the passage of a comprehensive education package as a clear political win, further supporting the expansion of social programs. The GI Bill unequivocally established the education benefits for returning service members (Pub. L. 78-346, 1944), which, given the scale of World War II, was a tremendous and long-lasting stimulus (Bound and Turner, 2002).

Third Era—the Modern Veteran Services System

After the Second World War, veterans' benefits continued to expand, with the modern VA system emerging in the Eisenhower administration (Ridgway, 2013). Since the VA's founding in the Hoover administration, there has been tension between keeping veteran programs distinct and integrating their services into the larger social service apparatus (Burtin, 2020a). The Eisenhower administration considered many VA programs duplicative and limited a unified federal social services system, increasing service delivery costs (Burtin, 2020a). The Bradley Report in 1956 recommended a series of focusing reforms designed to narrow what benefits could be provided by the VA. The veterans' organizations and community rallied and effectively lobbied Congress to limit the President's authority to make unilateral changes to the VA by formalizing it as statutory law in 1957 (Eisenhower, 1955).

Legislation passed by Congress in 1958 set the foundations of the modern VA system. As with other social services agencies, reforms and cost-adjustment measures continue to shape the VA. However, the demand for services from veterans also shaped the services provided by the VA and its role within the P3 ecosystem. The P3 ecosystem has always been a mixture of formal (state and federal programs) and informal (community, private, and nonprofit organizations), and the VA, within that P3 context, exemplifies how the push and pull from veteran advocacy and community engagement acted as a driver for social and institutional reform.

Punctuated Equilibrium Theory

One approach is to view veteran service movements as expressions of *demand* for government services and the government's provision of services as *supply*. The P3 ecosystem can be seen as an equilibrium between supply and demand. Unlike a classic microeconomic model, the VA's history shows periods of stable equilibrium interrupted by significant changes. The theory of *punctuated equilibrium*, which originated in ecology, public administration, and economics, helps explain this phenomenon (Green-Pedersen and Princen, 2016). It describes long periods of stability followed by large changes in service equilibrium. In this context, the x-axis represents the level of services (quantity), and the y-axis represents the net benefits of services (price), with equilibrium interactions between veterans' demand for services and the government's willingness to supply them. As Lipsky (2010) notes, the demand for government services in the social service regime seems infinite, but for veterans, it is limited to the number of qualifying veterans. Therefore, the demand for veteran services depends on the number of veterans seeking services. The supply of services is based on the cost-benefit trade-off in the political economy of the administrative state. This can be seen as the net present value of maintaining a dual-service system that duplicates some functions of other social service agencies. Thus, supply depends on the government's willingness to pay for an additional unit of veteran-focused service. The political economy of supply reflects the willingness of the people, expressed through their political representatives and the administrative state's implementation. An equilibrium occurs when there is sufficient political pressure and veteran service demand, prompting the government to fund additional services. Punctuated equilibrium theory suggests that major changes (punctuations) occur when demand for veteran services increases and the willingness to pay rises within the political and administrative elements of the government. These changes often follow major conflicts, when national appreciation for veterans, reflected by political officials, leads to increased demand for services (Figure H.1). This results in a shift in the level of service equilibrium.

Exploring the relationship between the federal government and nonprofit organizations from this perspective yields some interesting insights. There is a coproduced relationship between the veterans' groups and the formal federal service institutions, with the willingness to pay for services and the demand for those services reflected in the level of service. There is a duality in the role that veteran organizations play in the VA's P3 ecosystem. Not only do they help signal service demands, but they also support the development of new services at a micro-scale. This can be seen in the early history of the VA; for example, the American Legion helped propose and support the development of the GI Bill.

Furthermore, these organizations are often community-driven, seeking to express demand when a problem exceeds the community or state capacity to address the issue. Thus,

FIGURE H.1
Punctuated Equilibrium Model View

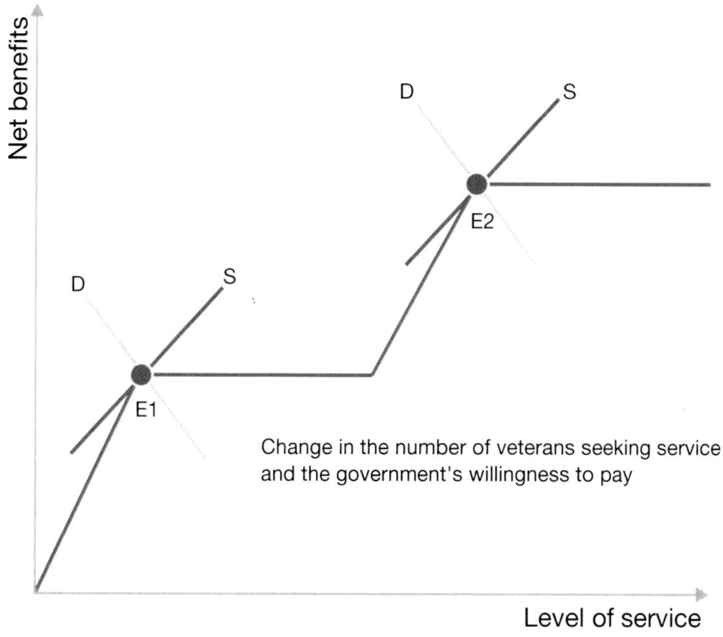

NOTE: D = demand; E = equilibrium; S = supply.

demand is expressed at the national level when there is a broader or more pressing social issue, such as the need for systematic health care or structured financial payments. The role of the P3 both in the delivery of services and as a social mobilizer is critical in meeting the needs of this country's veterans.

Abbreviations

9/11	the terrorist attacks of September 11, 2001
ACP	American Corporate Partners
AI/AN/Asian/PI	American Indian, Alaska Native, Asian, or Pacific Islander
ALP	American Life Panel
CNAS	Center for a New American Security
COVID-19	coronavirus disease 2019
DAV	Disabled American Veterans
DoD	U.S. Department of Defense
DoL	U.S. Department of Labor
ENPP	Employment Navigator and Partnership Program
FDR	Franklin Delano Roosevelt
FY	fiscal year
GAO	U.S. Government Accountability Office
HOH	Hiring Our Heroes
IRS	Internal Revenue Service
NOFO	Notice of Funding Opportunity
NTEE	National Taxonomy of Exempt Entities
O2O	Onward to Opportunity
P3	public-private partnership
PVA	Paralyzed Veterans of America
TAP	Transition Assistance Program
U.S. VETS	United States Veterans Initiative
VA	U.S. Department of Veterans Affairs
Vet Tix	Veteran Tickets Foundation
VFW	Veterans of Foreign Wars of the United States
VSO	veterans service organization
WIOA	Workforce Innovation Opportunity Act
WWP	Wounded Warrior Project

References

Abdel-Samad, Mounah, Jerel P. Calzo, Jennifer K. Felner, Lianne Urada, Matthew E. Verbyla, Hala Madanat, Brian E. Adams, Thais Alves, Bruce Appleyard, Joshua Chanin, Shawn Flanigan, Hisham Foad, Maya Ginsberg, Matthew Higgins, Eunjeong Ko, Kristen Maher, Natalie Mladenov, Peggy Peattie, Megan Welsh, and David Sleet, "Conceptualizing an Interdisciplinary Collective Impact Approach to Examine and Intervene in the Chronic Cycle of Homelessness," *International Journal of Environmental Research and Public Health*, Vol. 18, No. 4, 2021.

ACP—*See* American Corporate Partners.

Adler, Jessica L., *Burdens of War: Creating the United States Veterans Health System*, JHU Press, 2017.

Altman, Morris, "Behavioral Economics, Economic Theory and Public Policy," *Economic Theory and Public Policy*, June 27, 2008.

Altschuler, Glenn, and Stuart Blumin, *The GI Bill: The New Deal for Veterans*, Oxford University Press, 2009.

American Corporate Partners, "ACP Helps Veterans and Spouses Find Their Next Careers," webpage, undated. As of August 19, 2024:
https://www.acp-usa.org/

American Legion, "By the Numbers," webpage, undated. As of October 22, 2024:
https://register.legion.org/bythenumbers

Bank of America, "Giving with Purpose: How Affluent Households Contributed in 2022," webpage, 2023. As of August 19, 2024:
https://www.privatebank.bankofamerica.com/articles/2023-bank-of-america-study-of-philanthropy.html

Barrera, Cathy, and Phillip Carter, *Challenges on the Home Front: Underemployment Hits Veterans Hard*, Call of Duty Endowment and ZipRecruiter, 2017.

Beall, Jo, Zegeye Cherenet, Liza Cirolia, Nuno Da Cruz, Susan Parnell, and Philipp Rode, "Understanding Infrastructure Interfaces: Common Ground for Interdisciplinary Urban Research?" *Journal of the British Academy*, Vol. 7, No. 2, 2019.

Bennett, Jesse, "Veteran Households in U.S. Are Economically Better Off Than Those of Non-Veterans," Pew Research Center, December 9, 2019. As of August 19, 2024:
https://www.pewresearch.org/short-reads/2019/12/09/
veteran-households-in-u-s-are-economically-better-off-than-those-of-non-veterans/

Berglass, Nancy, and Margaret C. Harrell, *Well After Service: Veteran Reintegration and American Communities*, Center for a New American Security, April 2012. As of August 19, 2024:
https://www.cnas.org/publications/reports/
well-after-service-veteran-reintegration-and-american-communities

Black Veterans for Social Justice, *Financial Statements and Independent Auditors' Report Years Ended December 31, 2020 and 2019*, December 2020.

Boardman, Anthony E., and Aidan R Vining, "Assessing the Economic Worth of Public–Private Partnerships," in *International Handbook on Public–Private Partnerships*, Edward Elgar Publishing, 2010.

Bodenger, Robert George, *Soldiers' Bonuses: A History of Veterans' Benefits in the United States, 1776–1967*, The Pennsylvania State University, 1971.

Bound, John, and Sarah Turner, "Going to War and Going to College: Did World War II and the GI Bill Increase Educational Attainment for Returning Veterans?" *Journal of Labor Economics*, Vol. 20, No. 4, 2002.

Burtin, Olivier, "The History of Veterans' Policy in the United States," *Historical Social Research/Historische Sozialforschung*, Vol. 45, No. 2, 2020a.

Burtin, Olivier, "Veterans as a Social Movement: The American Legion, the First Hoover Commission, and the Making of the American Welfare State," *Social Science History*, Vol. 44, No. 2, 2020b.

Call of Duty Endowment, *2022 Annual Report*, undated.

Campbell, Alec, "The Sociopolitical Origins of the American Legion," *Theory and Society*, Vol. 39, 2010.

Candid, "GuideStar: Providing You with the Nonprofit Information You Need," webpage, undated. As of August 19, 2024:
https://www.guidestar.org/

Cao, Yongchao, Huimin Li, and Limin Su, "A Dynamic Performance-Based Payment Mechanism for Public-Private Partnership Projects: An Integrated Model for Principal-Agent and Multi-Objective Optimization Models," *International Journal of Strategic Property Management*, Vol. 28, No. 2, 2024.

Carter, Phillip, Amy Schafer, Katherine Kidder, and Moira Fagan, *Lost in Translation: The Civil-Military Divide and Veteran Employment*, Center for a New American Security, June 2017. As of August 19, 2024:
https://www.cnas.org/publications/reports/lost-in-translation

Center for Naval Analyses, *Population Representation in the Military Services: Fiscal Year 2019 Summary Report*, DRM-2021-U-029312, 2021.

Chairman's Office of Reintegration, "After the Sea of Goodwill: A Collective Approach to Veteran Reintegration," white paper, Office of the Chairman of the Joint Chiefs of Staff, October 2014.

Cimbala, Paul A., *Veterans North and South: The Transition from Soldier to Civilian After the American Civil War*, Bloomsbury Publishing USA, 2015.

Congressional Budget Office, *Transitioning from the Military to the Civilian Workforce: The Role of Unemployment Compensation for Ex-Servicemembers*, May 2017.

Congressional Budget Office, *Income of Working-Age Veterans Receiving Disability Compensation*, December 1, 2023.

Copeland, John W., and David W. Sutherland, "Sea of Goodwill: Matching the Donor to the Need," white paper, Office of the Chairman of the Joint Chiefs of Staff, Warrior and Family Support, 2010.

DAV—*See* Disabled American Veterans.

Davenport, Katie E., Nicole R. Morgan, Kimberly J. McCarthy, Julia A. Bleser, Keith R. Aronson, and Daniel F. Perkins, "The Subjective Underemployment Experience of Post-9/11 Veterans After Transition to Civilian Work," *Work*, Vol. 72, No. 4, August 11, 2022.

Deaton, A., and N. Cartwright, "Understanding and Misunderstanding Randomized Controlled Trials," *Social Science and Medicine*, August 2018.

Deterding, Nicole M., and Mary C. Waters, "Flexible Coding of In-Depth Interviews: A Twenty-First-Century Approach," *Sociological Methods & Research*, Vol. 50, No. 2, 2021.

Disabled American Veterans, *Keeping Our Promise to America's Veterans: 2022 Annual Report*, 2022.

DoD—*See* U.S. Department of Defense.

Edwards, Kathryn A., *Benchmarks for Success: Expected Short- and Long-Term Outcomes of National Guard Youth ChalleNGe Participants*, RAND Corporation, RR-A271-1, 2020. As of May 23, 2024:
https://www.rand.org/pubs/research_reports/RRA271-1.html

Eisenhower, Dwight D., "Letter to General Omar N. Bradley, Chairman, President's Commission on Veterans' Pensions, Concerning a Study of Veterans' Benefits," published online by Gerhard Peters and John T. Woolley, The American Presidency Project, March 5, 1955. As of August 22, 2024:
https://www.presidency.ucsb.edu/node/234032

ETS Sponsorship, "Program Overview," last updated November 28, 2021. As of August 19, 2024:
https://etssponsorship.com/data/get/613

Fausold, Martin L, *The Presidency of Herbert C. Hoover*, Vol. 11, University Press of Kansas, 1985.

FourBlock, "About," webpage, undated. As of August 19, 2024:
https://fourblock.org/about

FourBlock Foundation, *FourBlock Veteran Career Readiness: 2022 Annual Report*, undated.

Funnell, S. C., and P. J. Rogers, *Purposeful Program Theory: Effective Use of Theories of Change and Logic Models*, Wiley, 2011.

Gallouj, Camal, "Asymmetry of Information and the Service Relationship: Selection and Evaluation of the Service Provider," *International Journal of Service Industry Management*, Vol. 8, No. 1, 1997.

Galvin, Peter, Stephane Tywoniak, and Janet Sutherland, "Collaboration and Opportunism in Megaproject Alliance Contracts: The Interplay Between Governance, Trust and Culture," *International Journal of Project Management*, Vol. 39, Issue 4, 2021.

GAO—*See* U.S. Government Accountability Office.

Garamone, Jim, "Vice Chiefs Talk Recruiting Shortfalls, Readiness Issues," DOD News, April 20, 2023. As of August 22, 2024:
https://www.defense.gov/News/News-Stories/Article/article/3369472/vice-chiefs-talk-recruiting-shortfalls-readiness-issues/

Gaumer, Lynn M., "Giving USA 2023: Inside the Numbers and a Look Ahead," *Stelter Insights* blog, June 20, 2023. As of August 19, 2024:
https://blog.stelter.com/2023/06/20/giving-usa-2023-inside-the-numbers-and-a-look-ahead/

Gentzkow, Matthew, Bryan Kelly, and Matt Taddy, "Text as Data," *Journal of Economic Literature*, Vol. 57, No. 3, 2019.

Giving USA, "Giving USA 2017: Total Charitable Donations Rise to New High of $390.05 Billion," press release, June 12, 2017. As of August 19, 2024:
https://givingusa.org/giving-usa-2017-total-charitable-donations-rise-to-new-high-of-390-05-billion/

Green-Pedersen, Christoffer, and Sebastiaan Princen, "Punctuated Equilibrium Theory," *Handbook of Public Policy Agenda Setting*, Edward Elgar Publishing, 2016.

Grimmer, Justin, Margaret E. Roberts, and Brandon M. Stewart, *Text as Data: A New Framework for Machine Learning and the Social Sciences*, Princeton University Press, 2022.

Grossman, Sanford J., and Oliver D. Hart, "An Analysis of the Principal-Agent Problem," in *Foundations of Insurance Economics: Readings in Economics and Finance*, Springer, 1992.

Guo, Chao, and Muhittin Acar, "Understanding Collaboration Among Nonprofit Organizations: Combining Resource Dependency, Institutional, and Network Perspectives," *Nonprofit and Voluntary Sector Quarterly*, Vol. 34, No. 3, 2005.

Helmus, Todd C., Ryan Andrew Brown, and Rajeev Ramchand, *Prevalence of Veteran Support for Extremist Groups and Extremist Beliefs: Results from a Nationally Representative Survey of the U.S. Veteran Community*, RAND Corporation, RR-A1071-2-v2, 2023. As of April 18, 2024: https://www.rand.org/pubs/research_reports/RRA1071-2-v2.html

Herd, Pamela, and Donald P. Moynihan, *Administrative Burden: Policymaking by Other Means*, Russell Sage Foundation, 2019.

Hire Heroes USA, "It's All in the Numbers," webpage, undated. As of August 19, 2024: https://www.hireheroesusa.org/

Hire Heroes USA, *The Hire Heroes 2022 Report*, 2022.

Hiring Our Heroes, *Veterans in the Workplace 2023*, U.S. Chamber of Commerce Foundation, 2023. As of August 19, 2024: https://www.hiringourheroes.org/resources/veterans-in-the-workplace-2023/

HOH—*See* Hiring Our Heroes.

Hoover, Herbert, Executive Order 5398—Consolidation and Coordination of Governmental Activities Affecting Veterans, July 21, 1930. As of August 22, 2024: https://www.presidency.ucsb.edu/node/276053

Hunt, Nigel, and Ian Robbins, "World War II Veterans, Social Support, and Veterans' Associations," *Aging and Mental Health*, Vol. 5, No. 2, 2001.

Huston, Wendell, "Lapsed Insurance Under the World War Veterans Act," *American Bar Association Journal*, Vol. 11, No. 11, 1925.

Ilhan, Habibe, "Non Profit Organizations as Providers of Public Goods," *Journal of Management and Economics/Yönetim ve Ekonomi*, Vol. 20, No. 1, 2013.

Internal Revenue Service, *Tax Guide for Veterans' Organizations*, Publication 3386, Catalog Number 27489D, Rev. 4, 2018.

Internal Revenue Service, "Charitable Organizations," webpage, updated December 4, 2023a. As of January 9, 2024: https://www.irs.gov/charities-non-profits/charitable-organizations

Internal Revenue Service, "Exempt Organization Public Disclosure and Availability Requirements," webpage, updated December 4, 2023b. As of January 9, 2024: https://www.irs.gov/charities-non-profits/exempt-organization-public-disclosure-and-availability-requirements

Internal Revenue Service, "Veterans' Organizations," webpage, updated December 4, 2023c. As of August 19, 2024: https://www.irs.gov/charities-non-profits/other-non-profits/veterans-organizations

Iossa, Elisabetta, and David Martimort, "The Simple Microeconomics of Public-Private Partnerships," *Journal of Public Economic Theory*, Vol. 17, No. 1, 2015.

IRS—*See* Internal Revenue Service.

Karre, J. K., D. F. Perkins, N. R. Morgan, K. E. Davenport, K. R. Aronson, R. V. Maury, D. Bradbard, N. J. Armstrong, A. Wright, R. Sargent, and M. Andros, "What Do Successful Military-to-Civilian Transitions Look Like? A Revised Framework and a New Conceptual Model for Assessing Veteran Well-Being," *Armed Forces & Society*, 2024.

Kelly, Patrick J., *Creating a National Home: Building the Veterans' Welfare State, 1860–1900*, Harvard University Press, 1997.

Kingma, Bruce R., "Public Good Theories of the Non-Profit Sector: Weisbrod Revisited," *Voluntas: International Journal of Voluntary and Nonprofit Organizations*, Vol. 8, No. 2, 1997.

Kleykamp, Meredith, Crosby Hipes, and Alair MacLean, "Who Supports U.S. Veterans and Who Exaggerates Their Support?" *Armed Forces & Society*, Vol. 44, No. 1, 2018.

Kleykamp, Meredith, Daniel Schwam, and Gilad Wenig, *What Americans Think About Veterans and Military Service: Findings from a Nationally Representative Survey*, RAND Corporation, RR-A1363-7, 2023. As of August 19, 2024:
https://www.rand.org/pubs/research_reports/RRA1363-7.html

Kleykamp, Meredith, Jeffrey B. Wenger, Elizabeth Hastings Roer, Matthew Kubasak, Travis Hubble, and Lauren Skrabala, *Federal Programs to Assist Military-to-Civilian Employment Transitions*, RAND Corporation, RR-A1363-12, 2024. As of August 22, 2024:
https://www.rand.org/pubs/research_reports/RRA1363-12.html

Knowlton, Lisa Wyatt, and Cynthia C. Phillips, *The Logic Model Guidebook: Better Strategies for Great Results*, Sage Publications, 2009.

Koob, A., "Key Facts on U.S. Nonprofits and Foundations," Candid, 2021.

Kuzminski, Katherine L., and Phillip Carter, *Charting the Sea of Goodwill*, Center for a New American Security, December 9, 2015. As of August 19, 2024:
https://www.cnas.org/publications/reports/charting-the-sea-of-goodwill

Lambert, Richard A., Christian Leuz, and Robert E. Verrecchia, "Information Asymmetry, Information Precision, and the Cost of Capital," *Review of Finance*, Vol. 16, No. 1, 2012.

Liang, Yunping, and Baabak Ashuri, "Challenges and Enabling Features of Small and Medium Infrastructure Public-Private Partnerships (P3s): A Case Study of the US P3 Infrastructure Market," *Engineering, Construction and Architectural Management*, Vol. 29, No. 1, 2022.

Lilly Family School of Philanthropy, "Charitable Giving by Affluent Households Above Pre-Pandemic Levels," webpage, 2023a. As of August 19, 2024:
https://philanthropy.indianapolis.iu.edu/news-events/news/_news/2023/Charitable%20Giving%20by%20Affluent%20Households%20Above%20Pre-Pandemic%20Levels,%20Finds%202023%20Bank%20of%20America%20Study%20of%20Philanthropy.html

Lilly Family School of Philanthropy, "Giving USA: Total U.S. Charitable Giving Declined in 2022 to $499.33 Billion Following Two Years of Record Generosity," webpage, June 20, 2023b. As of August 22, 2024:
https://philanthropy.indianapolis.iu.edu/news-events/news/_news/2023/giving-usa-total-us-charitable-giving-declined-in-2022-to-49933-billion-following-two-years-of-record-generosity.html

LinkedIn, *2023 Veterans Opportunity Report*, 2023.

Lipsky, Michael, *Street-Level Bureaucracy: Dilemmas of the Individual in Public Service*, Russell Sage Foundation, 2010.

Loughran, David S., *Why Is Veteran Unemployment So High?* RAND Corporation, RR-284, 2014. As of July 31, 2024:
https://www.rand.org/pubs/research_reports/RR284.html

McCabe, Malia, "71 Charitable Giving Statistics You Need to Know in 2023," webpage, DealAid, January 2, 2023. As of August 19, 2024:
https://dealaid.org/research/charitable-giving/

McCormick, Doublas, Emma Moore, and Andrew Swick, "Changing Tides in the Sea of Goodwill: A Financial Analysis of Veteran-Serving Nonprofits," working paper, Center for a New American Security, 2018.

McEntarfer, Erika, "How Do Recent Veterans Fare in the Labor Market? New Census Bureau Data Show Diverse Outcomes for Recent Army Veterans," webpage, U.S. Census Bureau, July 8, 2020. As of August 19, 2024:
https://www.census.gov/library/stories/2020/07/how-do-recent-veterans-fare-in-the-labor-market.html

Military OneSource, "2022 Demographics Dashboards," undated. As of August 19, 2024:
https://demographics.militaryonesource.mil/chapter-2-personnel-separations

Millenky, Megan, Dan Bloom, Sara Muller-Ravett, and Joseph Broadus, *Staying on Course: Three-Year Results of the National Guard Youth ChalleNGe Evaluation*, MDRC, 2011.

Miller, Gary J., and Andrew B. Whitford, "The Principal's Moral Hazard: Constraints on the Use of Incentives in Hierarchy," *Journal of Public Administration Research and Theory*, Vol. 17, No. 2, 2007.

Moore, Emma, Margaret Seymour, Jared Stefani, Kelly Kennedy, and Kayla M. Williams, *Funding Flows in the Sea of Goodwill: An Analysis of Major Funders in the Veteran-Serving Nonprofit Space*, Center for a New American Security, 2019.

Moore, Mark A., and Aidan R. Vining, "PPP Performance Evaluation: The Social Welfare Goal, Principal-Agent Theory and Political Economy," *Policy Sciences*, Vol. 56, No. 2, 2023.

Murphy, Timothy J., "The Case for Public-Private Partnerships in Infrastructure," *Canadian Public Administration*, Vol. 51, No. 1, 2008.

"National Guard ChalleNGe Project," webpage, RAND Corporation, undated. As of August 29, 2024:
https://www.rand.org/nsrd/projects/national-guard-challenge.html

National Guard Youth ChalleNGe, "About the Program," webpage, undated. As of August 29, 2024:
https://ngchallenge.org/about-us/

Ortiz, Stephen R., B*eyond the Bonus March and GI Bill: How Veteran Politics Shaped the New Deal Era*, New York University Press, 2009a.

Ortiz, Stephen R., "3. The 'New Deal' for Veterans," in *Beyond the Bonus March and GI Bill*, New York University Press, 2009b.

Parker, Kim, Ruth Igielnik, Amanda Barroso, and Anthony Cilluffo, "Chapter 3: The Transition to Post-Military Employment," in *The American Veteran Experience and the Post-9/11 Generation*, Pew Research Center, September 10, 2019. As of August 19, 2024:
https://www.pewresearch.org/social-trends/2019/09/10/the-transition-to-post-military-employment/

Pencak, William, "American Veterans' Movements," in James C. Bradford, ed., *A Companion to American Military History*, Vol. 2, Wiley-Blackwell, 2009.

Perez-Arce, Francisco, Louay Constant, David S. Loughran, and Lynn A. Karoly, *A Cost- Benefit Analysis of the National Guard Youth ChalleNGe Program*, RAND Corporation, TR-1193-NGYF, 2012. As of August 29, 2024:
http://www.rand.org/pubs/technical_reports/TR1193.html

Perkins, Daniel F., and Nicole R. Mogan, "Military Sexual Trauma, Adverse Childhood Experiences, and Combat Exposure Among Female and Male Veterans and Successful Transition," online presentation, June 22, 2023.

PNC Financial Services Group, "Giving USA's 2022 Philanthropy Report," September 28, 2023.

Pollard, Michael S., and Matthew D. Baird, *The RAND American Life Panel: Technical Description,* RAND Corporation, RR-1651, 2017. As of August 19, 2024:
https://www.rand.org/pubs/research_reports/RR1651.html

ProPublica, "ETS Sponsorship Program," webpage, updated January 8, 2024a. As of January 9, 2024:
https://projects.propublica.org/nonprofits/organizations/843788971/202200669349201100/full

ProPublica, "U.S. Chamber of Commerce Foundation," webpage, updated January 8, 2024b. As of January 9, 2024:
https://projects.propublica.org/nonprofits/organizations/461561597/202243159349302579/full

Public Law 78–346, Servicemen's Readjustment Act of 1944, June 22, 1944.

Public Law 113-128, Workforce Innovation Opportunity Act, July 22, 2014.

Public Law 115-232, John S. McCain National Defense Authorization Act for Fiscal Year 2019, August 13, 2018. As of August 20, 2024:
https://www.govinfo.gov/app/details/PLAW-115publ232

Rachwalski, Maurice D., and Thomas W. Ross, "Running a Government's P3 Program: Special Purpose Agency or Line Departments?" *Journal of Comparative Policy Analysis: Research and Practice*, Vol. 12, No. 3, 2010.

Ridgway, James D., "Recovering an Institutional Memory: The Origins of the Modern Veterans' Benefits System from 1914 to 1958," *Veterans Law Review*, Vol. 5, 2013.

Rolen, Emily, "A Closer Look at Veterans in the Labor Force," *Career Outlook*, U.S. Bureau of Labor Statistics, November 2017. As of August 19, 2024:
https://www.bls.gov/careeroutlook/2017/article/veterans.htm

Roller, Scott, "PAServes—Greater Pittsburgh Best in U.S. for Connecting Returning Veterans with Essential Services," press release, The Heinz Endowments, March 5, 2020.

Romaniuk, Madeline, Gina Fisher, Matthew Sunderland, and Philip J. Batterham, "Development and Psychometric Evaluation of the Mental Readiness for Military Transition Scale (MT-Ready)," *BMC Psychiatry*, Vol. 23, No. 575, 2023.

Ross, Stephen A., "The Economic Theory of Agency: The Principal's Problem," *American Economic Review*, Vol. 63, No. 2, 1973.

Rybnicek, Robert, Julia Plakolm, and Lisa Baumgartner, "Risks in Public–Private Partnerships: A Systematic Literature Review of Risk Factors, Their Impact and Risk Mitigation Strategies," *Public Performance and Management Review*, Vol. 43, No. 5, 2020.

Schwam, Daniel, and James V. Marrone, *Veterans' Employment During Recessions: Veterans' Issues in Focus*, RAND Corporation, PE-A1363-7, 2023. As of August 19, 2024: https://www.rand.org/pubs/perspectives/PEA1363-7.html

Silaghi, Florina, and Sudipto Sarkar, "Agency Problems in Public-Private Partnerships Investment Projects," *European Journal of Operational Research*, Vol. 290, No. 3, 2021.

Smith, Steven Rathgeb, and Michael Lipsky, *Nonprofits for Hire: The Welfare State in the Age of Contracting*, Harvard University Press, 2009.

Stanley, Ian H., Carol Chu, Sarah M. Gildea, Irving H. Hwang, Andrew J. King, Chris J. Kennedy, Alex Luedtke, Brian P. Marx, Robert O'Brien, Maria V. Petukhova, et al., "Predicting Suicide Attempts Among U.S. Army Soldiers After Leaving Active Duty Using Information Available Before Leaving Active Duty: Results from the Study to Assess Risk and Resilience in Servicemembers–Longitudinal Study (STARRS-LS)," *Molecular Psychiatry*, Vol. 27, 2022.

Stevens, Rosemary, *A Time of Scandal: Charles R. Forbes, Warren G. Harding, and the Making of the Veterans Bureau*, JHU Press, 2016.

Syracuse University, "Onward to Opportunity (O2O) Impact Evaluation," webpage, undated-a. As of August 20, 2024: https://ivmf.syracuse.edu/article/onward-to-opportunity-o2o-impact-evaluation/

Syracuse University, "PAServes—About," webpage, undated-b. As of August 20, 2024: https://ivmf.syracuse.edu/programs/community-services/americaserves/locations/paserves/about/

Syracuse University, "The Employment Situation of Veterans—January 2024," webpage, 2024. As of August 21, 2024: https://ivmf.syracuse.edu/article/employment-situation-of-veterans-january-2024

Talavera, Carmen, and Joan R. Sanchis, "Alliances Between For-Profit and Non-Profit Organizations as an Instrument to Implement the Economy for the Common Good," *Sustainability*, Vol. 12, No. 22, 2020.

Tamborini, Christopher R., and Patrick J. Purcell, "Female Veterans: Socioeconomic Characteristics and Disability Patterns Among Social Security Beneficiaries," *Social Security Bulletin*, Vol. 83, No. 2, 2023. As of August 20, 2024: https://www.ssa.gov/policy/docs/ssb/v83n2/v83n2p1.html

Tipu, Waseem Ali, and Talha Yousaf, "Agency Theory in Public-Private Partnership Projects," *Administrative and Management Sciences Journal*, Vol. 1, No. 1, 2022.

Tucker, Spencer C., *The Encyclopedia of the Mexican-American War: A Political, Social, and Military History*, Bloomsbury Publishing USA, 2012.

U.S. Bureau of Labor Statistics, "Employment Situation of Veterans—2011," news release, USDL-12-0493, March 20, 2012.

U.S. Bureau of Labor Statistics, "Unemployment Among Veterans of the U.S. Armed Forces Declines in 2012," *TED: The Economics Daily*, March 22, 2013. As of August 20, 2024: https://www.bls.gov/opub/ted/2013/ted_20130322.htm

U.S. Bureau of Labor Statistics, "Employment Situation of Veterans—2022," news release, USDL23-0537, March 21, 2023.

U.S. Chamber of Commerce Foundation, "Hiring Our Heroes," webpage, undated. As of August 20, 2024: https://www.uschamberfoundation.org/solutions/workforce-development-and-training/hiring-our-heroes

U.S. Department of Labor, Employment and Training Administration, "Workforce Innovation and Opportunity Act," webpage, undated. As of August 23, 2024: https://www.dol.gov/agencies/eta/wioa

U.S. Department of Labor, Veterans' Employment and Training Service, "Employment Navigator and Partnership Program," webpage, undated. As of August 28, 2024: https://www.dol.gov/agencies/vets/programs/tap/employment-navigator-partnership

U.S. Department of Veterans Affairs, "Staff Sergeant Parker Gordon Fox Suicide Prevention Grant Program," webpage, updated September 20, 2023. As of January 9, 2024: https://www.mentalhealth.va.gov/ssgfox-grants/

U.S. Department of Veterans Affairs, "Veteran and Spouse Transitional Assistance Grant Program," 38 CFR Part 80, *Federal Register*, Vol. 89, No. 93, May 13, 2024. As of August 28, 2024: https://www.govinfo.gov/content/pkg/FR-2024-05-13/pdf/2024-09862.pdf

U.S. Department of Veterans Affairs, National Center for Healthcare Advancement and Partnerships, "Veteran Community Partnerships," webpage, updated January 17, 2024. As of August 28, 2024:
https://www.va.gov/healthpartnerships/vcp.asp

U.S. House of Representatives, Veterans Opportunity to Work Act, H.R. 2433, 112th Congress, 2011.

U.S. Government Accountability Office, *Servicemembers Transitioning to Civilian Life: DOD Can Better Leverage Performance Information to Improve Participation in Counseling Pathways*, GAO-23-104538, 2022. As of August 20, 2024:
https://www.gao.gov/products/gao-23-104538

U.S. Vets, "How We Serve," brochure, undated.

Urahn, Susan K., Erin Currier, Diana Elliott, Lauren Wechsler, Denise Wilson, and Daniel Colbert, *Pursuing the American Dream: Economic Mobility Across Generations*, Pew Charitable Trusts, July 1, 2012.

Urban Institute, "IRS Activity Codes," webpage, National Center for Charitable Statistics, January 22, 2019. As of August 20, 2024:
https://nccs.urban.org/publication/irs-activity-codes

VA—*See* U.S. Department of Veterans Affairs.

"Veteran and Spouse Transitional Assistance Grant Program," webpage, FederalGrantsWire, undated. As of August 28, 2024:
https://www.federalgrantswire.com/veteran-and-spouse-transitional-assistance-grant-program-vstagp.html

Veteran Jobs Mission, "About the Mission," webpage, undated. As of August 20, 2024: https://www.veteranjobsmission.com/about-the-mission

VetJobs, "The Leader in Job Placement and Career Progression for our Military and Veteran Communities for 19 Years," webpage, undated. As of August 20, 2024:
https://vetjobs.org/

VetJobs, "2023 Military Community Impact Summary," 2024. As of October 22, 2024: https://vetjobs.org/impact-statement

Vining, Aidan R., Anthony E. Boardman, and Finn Poschmann, "Public-Private Partnerships in the US and Canada: 'There Are No Free Lunches,'" *Journal of Comparative Policy Analysis: Research and Practice*, Vol. 7, No. 3, 2005.

Ward, Shane, and Cathleen Clerkin, "The 990s Are Here. Why That's a Big Deal and What Happens Now," Candid blog, June 12, 2023. As of August 20, 2024: https://blog.candid.org/post/new-990s-are-here-why-thats-a-big-deal-what-happens-now/

Weisbrod, Burton, *The Nonprofit Economy*, Harvard University Press, 2009.

Wenger, Jennie W., Louay Constant, and Linda Cottrell, *National Guard Youth ChalleNGe: Program Progress in 2016–2017*, RAND Corporation, RR-2276-OSD, 2018. As of May 31, 2024: https://www.rand.org/pubs/research_reports/RR2276.html

White House, "About Joining Forces," webpage, undated. As of August 20, 2024: https://obamawhitehouse.archives.gov/joiningforces/about

Williamson, Oliver, and Scott Masten, *The Economics of Transaction Costs*, Edward Elgar Publishing, 1999.

Wilson, John R. M., "The Quaker and the Sword: Herbert Hoover's Relations with the Military," *Military Affairs: The Journal of Military History, Including Theory and Technology*, Vol. 38, No. 2, April 1974.

Wounded Warrior Project, "Your Dollars at Work: Financial Breakdown Data Compiled from FY 2022 IRS Form 990," undated. As of August 20, 2024: https://www.woundedwarriorproject.org/mission/financials/your-dollars-at-work

Wounded Warrior Project, *Annual Report Fiscal Year 2022*, 2023a.

Wounded Warrior Project, "Wounded Warrior Project Announces 2023–2024 Community Partnerships to Enhance Veteran Support," press release, October 24, 2023b. As of March 22, 2024: https://newsroom.woundedwarriorproject.org/2023-10-24-Wounded-Warrior-Project-Announces-2023-2024-Community-Partnerships-to-Enhance-Veteran-Support?_gl=1*570xkf*_ga*MTY3ODkwNDg2LjE3MDc5MzY2Nzg.*_ga_R4MM40GQC5*MTcxMTExNTg1OS4zLjEuMTcxMTExNTg4MC4zOS4wLjA

Wounded Warrior Project, *Annual Report Fiscal Year 2023*, 2024.

WWP—*See* Wounded Warrior Project.

Xiong, Wei, Xianbo Zhao, and Huanming Wang, "Information Asymmetry in Renegotiation of Public–Private Partnership Projects," *Journal of Computing in Civil Engineering*, Vol. 32, No. 4, 2018.